Mangia
Bevel
1

Ciro's
RESTAURANT AND LOUNGE

Si Mangia é Si Beve A Perfezione

THE FINEST IN ITALIAN AND AMERICAN CUISINE

2

Ciro's Restaurant

"To our Patrons"

Our ambition is to attend to your dining pleasure with such devotion that Ciros's Restaurant will automatically go on your preferred list.

All Dinners are cooked to order. Please be patient. Enjoy our cocktail bar.

Thank you.

Dedication

I dedicate my book, *Memories of Ciro's* to Dad, Aunt Rose, and Grandparents Al & Rose Scibelli. It was through their determination and working many long hours, which made Ciro's Restaurant the success it was. They "lived the dream," becoming successful Italian-American business owners for almost 30 years. To me, that is commendable. The original Ciro's Restaurant became an iconic location in the South End of Springfield Massachusetts and will never be forgotten.

This book has been bittersweet for me to write in many ways, having lost all of my immediate family, with the exception of my Aunt Rose Marconi and Cousin Alberto. My intention is not to bring sadness or tears when reading this memoir, although many of you may feel a tug at your heartstrings. What I hope is that you feel love, warmth, wonderful memories, and good times that can never ever be duplicated in any way. I pray the most important people who were once in my life, are now looking down upon me, as well as you, from up above smiling.

Acknowledgments

A very special thank you to the many people who helped make this book possible. I especially want to thank my husband John Mullin for all his support through the many months it has taken me to complete this tribute. I would also like to give a special thank you to my cousin Carla Sarno who talked to me through difficult moments, shedding light and different perspectives to me and offering me wonderful suggestions (and recipes) throughout this process.

I would also like to thank Sandra Vella for her knowledge of the South End, and expert advice on all things Italian, providing me with many ideas and offering support; and finally, to all my cousins, friends, and friends of my family who gave me their wonderful recollection of memories while in and around Ciro's. To all of you who contributed to the wonderful family recipe section, I thank you as well. I am filled with gratitude and love for each and every one of you.

Introduction

This book, *Memories of Ciro's*, was a pleasure for me to write. I have compiled some of the moments that have stood out in my mind, growing up in and around our Italian Restaurant located in Springfield, Massachusetts. The original thought for this book was written for my family who are still living. As time has gone by, I feel the need to share my very interesting story with all of you. The second half of this book will include many of our favorite family recipes. The inspiration to write this stemmed from a place in my heart, paying homage and respect to my Mom, Dad, Nonie, and Papa Scibelli.

The recipe section is specifically a tribute to Dad and Nonie, who with many years of cooking experience, learned to make the most delicious Italian food you ever tasted. Although not classically trained as chefs, cooking had become a passion for them and a very important part of their lives. They didn't do it for themselves, but always had others in mind, with much love from their hearts. In my opinion, this is one of the reasons I think the food always tasted especially good!

I have a very large extended family, with many cousins who so kindly and generously have chosen to give me some of their own recipes that they make to this day. They will also be listed in the recipe section of this book. Some of the recipes stem from creations that Ciro's used to make; others are their own spin on Italian classics or just recipes they have come to love to make.

I am honored to share this book with you. Many wonderful people played a tremendous role during the years that Ciro's was in operation. They always helped Nonie and Papa, whenever they were called upon. If they could help, they would be there. We were a tight knit Italian-American family.

In short, this book is a way to record the years gone by and the memories that are dear to me. Whenever I feel the need to be reconnected again or am feeling nostalgic, I go back to these years experienced at Ciro's.

I am an only child, with just one first cousin, Aunt Rose (Scibelli) Marconi's son, Alberto. We share many of the same memories. He is the closest thing to a brother I will ever have. But even though I was an only child, it never mattered because I was always surrounded by so many wonderful family relatives and friends. My grammar school and church, Our Lady of Mount Carmel, was right behind the restaurant, so I was always very close to my roots growing up.

In The Beginning…..

My family owned Ciro's, an Italian restaurant in the South End of Springfield, Massachusetts, for almost 30 years. It all began somewhere around 1965, but it quickly earned its reputation as one of the best Italian Restaurants in all of Western Mass and Northern Connecticut.

Papa or Albert (Big Al) as he was called and Nonie or Rose Scibelli (Mama Rose) purchased Ciro's Restaurant which was located at 870 Main Street in the South End of Springfield, MA. Originally it was a very small establishment, consisting of one bar, and 2 small dining rooms and of course, the kitchen. As time went on, and business began to increase, the restaurant eventually underwent renovations and expansions took place, the first one being when they took over 2 other small businesses adjoining the original restaurant.

Nonie and Papa were among the first in the neighborhood of the South End to make a financial investment and commitment, as their roots were firmly planted and they were very determined to make their dream a success. And they did.

When I say "family restaurant," I mean it. Over the years, many cousins, aunts, and uncles worked there. They were often called upon at the spur of the moment to help out on a busy night. Nonie and Papa, along with my Dad Frankie, Aunt Rose (Baby Rose), and my Mother, Carol Lee, all worked at and ran the restaurant to some capacity.

Cousin Sandy Fragomeni recalls that from 1972-1982, she worked as a cocktail waitress in the lounge until she had her son Chris. The same went for cousin Diane King who worked roughly the same time as Sandy did, according to her daughter Mary-Ann. Dad would usually be found supervising the lounge and tending the bar. Cousin Anthony and his brother Albert Lattell worked quite a bit in the lounge as well as the "old bar' to help out.

 Aunt Rose, the hostess, was in charge of reservations and party seating. She made sure the entire wait staff was available and ready to serve at their stations. And let us not forget Aunt Rose's "famous Bleu Cheese dressing" that she made for the salads. It was the best! Actually, all the dressings at Ciro's were homemade. Nothing ever came out of a bottle or jar like so many other restaurants use. I personally loved our Classic Italian dressing for the salad that was hand tossed by Mom in a huge salad bowl. She premixed it in the kitchen, and then put each serving in bowls to be served to the patrons. On a busy night, she had all she could to keep up with making it!

Cousin Mary-Ann (King) DiPietro recalls several memories growing up around Ciro's. Mary-Ann and I are only a few years apart, and her brother Mike is a bit younger than us. She said that her favorite dish when she was a kid going to Ciro's was a tie between the Baked Ziti and the Chicken Parmesan, and of course the best Italian bread which was made by her Grandfather (my Uncle) Mario Settembro who owned the Italian Baking Company. He was married to Papa's sister, Carmella. His bakery was on the corner of the block. He supplied the bread to the restaurant for many years.

She recalls helping out as a young teenager hanging coats in the coat room on busy nights or holidays like Mother's Day. She said, "the best part was I was able to keep all the tips and I did pretty darn well!" There were nights when her mother Diane worked and her Grandfather Mario would babysit her and Mike. He would bring them over to Ciro's where they would sit in the lounge while her mother worked; he would sit and have a Scotch, and she would have a Shirley Temple! All of our family was around Ciro's, to some capacity.

Another cousin close to me in age was sometimes called upon to help out on a busy night or holiday event being held at Ciro's was cousin John Grondalski. He said, "I worked in the coat room once on a New Year's Eve. I was told I was stationed there to 'guard all the patrons' fur coats!" Customers used to come dressed up to the hilt, especially on an occasion where there would be a big evening filled with a set menu, then dancing and music afterward, like ringing in the New Year.

Mom, who gave up her career as a registered nurse, worked in the kitchen as I mentioned, but she also made the best antipastos in the world! The cold broccoli served with lemon, oil, and garlic was one of many favorite appetizers. As waitress Judi Daniele said, "People are still talking about the food at Ciro's and nothing will ever compare. The broccoli was the best. I would eat it on my break, and the funny thing is, as 'simple' as it may be to make, you just could not make broccoli like that at home! Strange but true." That cold broccoli was considered one of Ciro's famous dishes!

Judi still remembers Mom (Carol Lee) making the prettiest antipastos. "She used a half of iceberg lettuce upside down and made toothpick flowers out of various types of Italian salami and prosciutto and cheeses with all its accompaniments like marinated mushrooms, roasted red pepper strips, both black and green olives and spicy pickled pepperoncini." She emphasized that it was a "very special antipasto!"

To tell you what kind of "extended" family we have, they always did their best to help out. Believe me when I tell you there were many, many busy nights! I can remember being there on the weekend and seeing the line of hungry patrons waiting to get into Ciro's. This line literally went out the door and down the sidewalk in front of the restaurant. If you didn't have a reservation at least a week in advance, you had better be prepared to wait a very long time.

As many repeat customers would tell you, "it was always well worth the wait." So we never minded standing for what seemed like hours to get in. We also hosted many special holidays as I mentioned such as Mother's Day and New Year's Eve. Those special evenings would book out months in advance. There were special "seating" times and after dinner music and dancing.

Two of Papa's brothers, Uncles Tommy and Andrew "Edon" (Scibelli) also used to tend the "old bar" during the daytime hours before Ciro's opened for dinner. One of Papa's sisters, Auntie Clara (Scibelli) Fragomeni, was Nonie's office assistant. She helped Nonie with paying bills to vendors, doing general bookkeeping, and helping with payroll for employees.

It took a lot of loyalty, commitment, hard work, sweat, and many tears to make Ciro's the success that it was for so many years. I must say, Nonie was the heart and soul of that restaurant. It was she who motivated and pushed everyone to make it a success. They gave up everything to make that happen. She and Papa rarely took vacations or even took time off for that matter. Neither did Mom, Dad or Aunt Rose.

Once in a great while, we would all take a day or so, in the summertime to go to Milford, CT, to visit Aunt Celia and Uncle Sam Spagnoli. They had a house right on the beach. It was so nice to have the family together, outside of the hustle and bustle of being at Ciro's.

For a few summers, Nonie insisted that Mom and Dad take me on a vacation while she, Papa, and Aunt Rose tended Ciro's. So we would take a week or so to go to South Yarmouth on Cape Cod. We stayed at The Red Jacket Beach Resort. It was located right on the beach and was a very lovely, relaxing place. Mom always loved the sound of the ocean and sitting in the sun on the beach.

My family got to know the owners quite well over the years, and that was very nice. We always received "special accommodations" when we arrived. Dad and I would walk out into the ocean during low tide and dig for conchs. We also went fishing off the jetty and caught huge flounder. Dad would go into their kitchen and ask the chef if he would prepare it for us for dinner. He also knew the bartender, so we all would have a drink (me a Shirley temple) and chat with him before we went into the dining room to eat.

We all believed in being close to home, and it was fortunate that Ciro's was only 2 streets from Nonie and Papa's house in the South End of Springfield. They were able to walk over to the restaurant until the bad weather came. The only day "off" that everyone had was the day Ciro's was closed, Tuesday evenings. Even then, they would often be found at Ciro's preparing food for an upcoming party the next night or ordering food or alcohol to ensure there would be enough for the remainder of the week and especially for the busy weekend.

Many of the loyal employees, who were not "blood," were still considered "family" to Nonie and Papa. They all held a very special place in their hearts and meant a lot to them. They were very devoted to Ciro's and worked very hard to help make Ciro's the success that it had become. Waitresses such a Ginger Spinelli, Judy Daniele, Carol S, Ruthie, Inga and Karen Rossi were just a few of the wonderful people who worked there for many years.

Others would come and go after a short period of time for one reason or another, but they were all appreciated. I want those of you who are able to read this to know just how much "Big Al and Mama Rose" loved you! If they were alive today, they would personally thank you again for your dedication! So on their behalf, I take this opportunity to do so. Thank you!

Dad was lucky to have had so many friends throughout the years that would help him in many ways. As he would quote the phrase "one hand washes the other" so it was very true of Dad. He did many things for many people when they asked for his help. Dad was a very humble man, and if you had the pleasure of knowing him, you know he would take the "shirt off his back" if you asked. We all miss his charm and wit and let's face it, those of us who knew him, miss his wise cracks the most! I'm sure that's where I get it from!

There were also many chefs over the years who were personally trained by "Mama Rose." She taught them the recipes she knew and loved, showing them exactly how she wanted things to be prepared. Nonie was a perfectionist in every way! One of the first chefs employed there brought some very unique recipes. Nonie worked with him, exchanging thoughts and ideas that eventually led to the ones listed on her menu. By collaborating, they were able to create the dishes that Ciro's became famous for.

As one of the waitresses employed in the early 1990s, Karen Rossi reflected to me, "Mama Rose was a business owner, matriarch, South End of Springfield historian, Hostess for the city events, officials, performers, doctors, lawyers and judges, and was an amazing hard working Italian-American woman. Despite her ailments and decline of health as time went on, she always persevered and kept a positive outlook and spirit, which kept everyone going at Ciro's for as long as it did."

Once she and Papa were no longer physically able to run the restaurant to the capacity they wanted, things began to change. Their initiative and drive slowly declined, but their will and desire were still there. It just wasn't enough to keep the doors of Ciro's open much longer once this happened.

Papa had the same desire for success, working very hard, until that unfortunate day in 1980. It was Mom's wake. She was just 38 when she passed. For 3 long days and nights lines of family and friends came to pay their respect. Mom was an exceptional person in every way and was loved by many.

I remember looking over to where Papa was standing and noticed that he did not look well. At that moment, he had a massive stroke, at

Forestiere's Funeral Parlor, which left his speech partially impaired and one half of his body paralyzed. From that point on he was unable to perform the daily tasks he used to. Once he got some mobility back, walking with an arm crutch and a brace on his leg, he retired daily to his "seat" in the old bar. Unfortunately, he was never the same after the stroke. One thing that never changed with Papa I must say was his love for cigars. He always had one!

Things That Made Ciro's Unique.....

Into the 1970s, many celebrities and performers would frequent Ciro's. Many times Nonie would make special concessions and serve them well after the restaurant was closed for the evening and into the wee hours of the morning after these celebrities had finished their performances.

At the time there was a well-known pavilion called Storrowtown Theatre, which was located on the Fairgrounds of the Eastern States Exposition, also known as the "Big E." The performances usually took place in the evening, and it always was a "big affair," especially for me as a child and my cousin Alberto, who were able to attend these shows and afterward personally meet the performers in their dressing room trailers. These trailers were set up behind the arena, and those attending the show were not allowed in the back area, but we were.

Storrowtown was a lovely outdoor arena, seats in a circular pattern, under a big "tent" with the stage in the very center of it all. After our "visit" with the performers, we would all head down to Ciro's. The adults would set things up and get everything ready to serve the performers. By this time Ciro's was closed to regular patrons, as it was approaching between 11 pm or midnight by the time they arrived with their entourage.

Liberace the great pianist and flamboyant performer became a "regular" at Storrowton theater. My family got to know him over the years, and often we would have front row seats in the arena when he came to town. During his show, he always came out in full-length furs and heavily beaded costumes. He also loved to show off his gorgeous (and very large) diamond rings and jewelry. Nonie loved jewelry also, and she had some spectacular pieces of her own. Lee would often stop in the middle of his performance to engage with the audience and he always would mention Ciro's and say a few words to Nonie and Papa.

He would come to the edge of the stage and asked her if she had gotten any new jewelry and so they could "compare" the rings on their fingers. He actually would bend down so he could put his hand out to her, to show her his latest piece! She loved the attention and the fact that he took the time to talk to her during his show!

Liberace became a personal friend of Nonie and family, and it was a "given" to expect him at Ciro's after every one of his shows. If anyone had the opportunity to have had seen "Lee" (Liberace's first name), in person, he was just as flashy and funny off the stage too. We would be there until the wee hours of the morning, my cousin Alberto and I often asleep by that time, napping on one of the booths, after all the excitement of the evening!

Before Alberto and I could no longer keep our eyes open, we would sit down together with these performers and indulge in extravagant plates of food prepared for us. These are times I will never forget. Storrowton favorites such as Perry Como, Jerry Vale, Sandler and Young and many others frequented Ciro's after their shows and what an honor it was to serve them our food, and sit with them to enjoy it!

Many performers such as Englebert Humperdink, Tom Jones, Andre the Giant, Bobby Orr or Larry Bird would also visit Ciro's. They came to eat during regular business hours before their shows at the then Civic Center in Downtown Springfield. Today it is known at the Mass Mutual Center.

When special guests came, we discretely sat them in what we called the "moon booth." It was a half rounded booth, with chairs on the opposite side of the table. It was the most "private" area. The back of the booth was very high and faced outward. We tried our best not to "advertise" who was coming. We didn't want to cause too much of a crazy "fan" commotion! As you know, word travels and many people found out. This resulted in a very busy restaurant, but we certainly didn't mind!

If you were to walk into the lounge, Dad would have been very proud to show you all of the many awards, trophies, and citations from various agencies, community groups, touch football leagues, school sports, and elected officials. One of these that meant a great deal to my Dad was from the National Sudden Infant Death Syndrome (SIDS) Foundation. He made many contributions and supported these foundations. Others were from the Springfield Fire Department, Holyoke Boy's Club, Cathedral High School, and of course The South End Business Association. Dad was great for making donations and contributions in the name of Ciro's. Many of these organizations were in need or wanted "sponsorship, " and he was willing to help.

Our family also became friends with many political figures from the city such as former Mayors Theodore (Ted) Dimauro and William (Billy) Sullivan and his family. Others included Congressman Richard Neal, Representative Edward Boland, and former Governor Michael Dukakis. There were many prominent Doctors, Lawyers, and Judges from the city who frequented Ciro's too. A lot of these people were considered "regulars" because they had their own specific table or booth, along with special days and times when Ciro's was open. Aunt Rose always made sure the table(s) were set properly and reserved signs were visible, so no one sat at the tables that were awaiting them.

Nonie and Dad, being the generous people that they were always made a point to have a special "appetizer" on "the house" for them, and their favorite bottle of wine or cocktail that Dad made.

Nonie was very proud of her delicious recipes, and throughout the years, many people and chefs from various restaurants in the area would often try to duplicate them. Some would go as far as to be bold enough to ask her "just exactly what is in this dish?" She would always smile and tell them most of the ingredients, but never ever let all her secrets out.

We would often sit at the back table near her office in the restaurant and joke about it and laugh because many of these people thought they had figured it out! But no matter where we ate out at various competitor restaurants in the area (all of whom my family was personal friends with), we always knew they were trying to make the same tasting dish as she did, but they just couldn't replicate it exactly. This made her very happy.

We always enjoyed going to other popular restaurants on the one evening a week that Ciro's was closed. Places such as The Mountain Laurel Restaurant, which was in Enfield, CT; The Log Cabin; The Delaney House; The Riverboat; Monte Carlo; and Salvatore's to name a few. These were always special to have dinner. I remember getting very excited as a child because we would actually get dressed up and get to go out as a whole family for an evening of fun and great food. My family was friends with all the proprietors, and we were always treated with a little extra special consideration, just as we did for them, whether it was with a special dish that they prepared or an after dinner drink for the adults on "the house."

Ciro`s Restaurant circa 1965

Albert and Rose Scibelli in Ciro`s foyer

Frankie tending the bar 1970, aka :Shooter

Carol Lee`s RN graduation 1963

"Baby" Rose with Nonie 1996

Me and Auntie Clara Fragomeni

Frankie sharing a moment with his dad 1990

Cousin Alberto

Me and Nana Siemienkowicz.
Wolcott St.1990

One of my birthday in old Ciro`s

Frankie and his cousin Jim Langone

Mom, Dad, Papa old bar 1969

Carol Lee in Nonie`s old office 1971

Carol Lee working hard at the salad

26

Little Frankie circa 1950's

Frankie aka " Turtle" with buddies
creating mischief in the South End

Me and Dad behind Ciro's after school

Me and Alberto's Lounge Mural 1975

Infamous Blue Room 1980

Family head table, party in Blue Room

Lounge filled with family

"Mother`s Day" in
Springfield Newspaper

"Rene and his band" Ad in Springfield Newspaper

28

More extended family, Blue Room

Dad `teasing` me

Me and extended family, Blue Room

Party table with an array of La
Fiorentina`s pastries and cake

29

Gorgeous Ciro`s fruit display with Dad and cousin Mike Langone

Nonie, Papa and me, old Ciro`s 1968

Nana & Papa, Thanksgiving early 1990

30

Keep Your Friends Close, and Your Enemies Closer....

Anyone who lived in the Springfield area, especially in the South End and frequented Ciro's Restaurant in the late 1960s through the '80s knew of the presence of "Organized Crime." Many prominent figures could be found in and around Ciro's on any given day or evening. As a child it didn't mean much to me. Being around these people had little if any effect. I witnessed a few people in particular (who shall remain nameless) who always sat at a particular table always "reserved" just for them. They would eat and conduct their meetings for the evening.

Many times they would just sit in the lounge having a drink at one of the small tables inconspicuously discussing their business. It became old hat for me to see this. We all just went about our business. Dad tended the lounge, and Nonie would often be in her office paying vendors or writing checks for payroll. Aunt Rose, the wonderful hostess that she was, made sure the customers were seated in a timely manner.

I never asked questions regarding them, and if I did Dad would tell me it was none of my business. That would be the end of that conversation. I would never ask again. Dad would always be the first one to tell me, as you hear in a famous movie, "Keep

your mouth shut and never rat on your friends."
That was another one of his mottos. He believed it,
and he lived it.

It was funny because if you were to talk to any of
the permanent waitresses, they could tell you very
funny stories of how at least one of them in
particular would barge into the kitchen to demand
what exactly it was that he wanted to eat, and how
he wanted it prepared. If he didn't get what he
wanted, you could hear the yelling in the kitchen!
Not the best thing to be going on, on a busy
Saturday evening, but it was the way it was! One of
the waitresses, who was there when two particular
individuals from the organization even had their
own special "dinner plates" that only they ate off
of!

These individuals were always nice to me. They
were often there while we were celebrating for
birthday's and special occasions and were very
generous to me. I was always gracious, and was
told to say "thank you, " and I did.

Nonie was always accommodating to their needs as
was my Dad. Whatever they asked for, they got, to
the best of our ability. There wasn't a reason not to.
As we all know, if you ask a favor, expect to be
tapped on the shoulder at any time to repay it, and
my family was well aware of this. Dad always used

to say to me when I'd sit in the lounge with him, as I got older, "Just remember Laur, what comes around goes around." In other words, treat others as you want to be treated.

When Business was Booming…..

I remember as a child, walking over to the restaurant after school in the early afternoon. I attended Our Lady of Mount Carmel Grammar School and as I had previously mentioned it was located literally behind where the restaurant was. It was part of my daily routine to go there and wait for Dad to bring me home after school. There were times when I would have to wait for him for one reason or another, so I would have a soda and a snack from the old bar.

In those days, nobody thought anything about a minor walking behind the bar to get a soda. It was my family's restaurant, so it was OK! So, I just did it and didn't think twice! I still remember the thick black rubber non-skid mats to prevent falls behind the bar and the soda dispenser that I would get my Coca-Cola from so clearly. Small bags of chips and pretzels would be on a metal clip rack, and I just took what I wanted. I often sat right on the end at the bar. No questions asked or comments made. It was all very normal to all of us.

The restaurant would be empty, except for a few chefs that would be there to prep the ingredients and make sure everything would be ready for the upcoming busy evening. Food service didn't begin until 4pm. While I was waiting, it gave me the opportunity to run around the restaurant and play hide and seek with some of the chefs or staff that were taking a break from their prepping duties. Often cousin Alberto would be there and we would laugh and have so much fun.

When Dad took me home, it was to Nana's house located in the Hungry Hill section of Springfield. The four of us lived there (Mom, Dad, me and Nana). It was about a 10-minute ride by car to get to the South End where Ciro's was located, and it was very convenient. We lived with Nana the better part of my life growing up until my parents decided to purchase a home of their own, located in the Sixteen Acres section of Springfield, in the late 1970s.

Sometimes it was very hard for me when Mom was called into work on the one night she was supposed to have off, which was Mondays. I remember crying and being so upset because I was looking forward to spending time with her. Ciro's was so busy, and I had a hard time understanding why she had to leave me to go to work. She and Nana did the best they could to explain to me that it was very busy and they needed her to work. I was just a child.

Luckily, I had two best friends that lived close by. We would play and have sleepovers. Sherry

(Gerani) Mengal lived only a few doors down on Wolcott Street from me. My other childhood friend Cindy (Zguro) O'Brien lived on Leslie Street, the street above me. We spent a lot of time with each of them as we were growing up. Both of them to some capacity sharing milestones of mine like Birthdays and First Communion, etc. Sherry often came down to Ciro's to have dinner with Nana and me, and we always had a lot of jokes and laughs!

In 1974, Nonie and Papa decided to expand and renovate Ciro's. They purchased the adjoining businesses next door to them. They had the dream of turning the then "average" Italian restaurant, into an elegant place to dine. The quality of the food was always there, but now it was time to expand. Walls were knocked down and I recall discussions about how the layout of the new, larger room would be set up. Things like where the tables would be set, how many booths to put in, where the waitress station would be, and Nonie's new office would be. It was quite a task, and took quite a while to get everything right, as Nonie wanted everything 'just so.'

I still remember the stunning colors of black and red, with white table cloths and booths. There were gorgeous stainedglass window panels located in the front to the restaurant, also in the same colors. It was very typically "Italian" in many respects, but at the same time, very unique in design. The gigantic crystal chandelier that hung in the "original" now redone part of the dining room was just stunning. It's something people who frequented Ciro's will never forget it.

A unique feature that they had decided *not* to change was an exposed brick wall, which separated the main dining room from the lounge. It was beautiful, and people always commented on it. As you walked through the doorway from the brick wall into the lounge, all you saw were the exquisite red leather high back chairs, with black tables, large mirrors against the wall and red woven leather high back swivel bar stools.

At the back of the room was a canvas mural, painted by a local artist. It was a painting of me with Cousin Alberto in front of me, holding an apple in his hand. I used to have to sit behind Ciro's once I was out of Mt. Carmel School for the day with Dad. The artist would take many photos. He was trying to capture a certain look, which eventually would be used for the mural.

Customers always commented on how lovely it was to Dad. As Alberto and I grew up, many patrons commented on how much we still resembled the mural. That piece of canvas on the wall was always special to us.

In 1978, my Grandparents made the decision to purchase the remaining business that would allow them to own the whole block on Main Street in the South End of Springfield for the expansion of their idea to open a banquet room, the infamous "Blue Room." It was equipped with its own kitchen, Dad spending many afternoons just making things for us like his famous sauce and dishes like beef rollatini called braciole. Whatever he felt like making, he made. It was always a surprise to walk into the back kitchen and I remember walking very often into that kitchen of the Blue Room to pay him a visit. I could smell the aromas of his wonderful homemade sauce before I even entered the lounge. I'd walk in to find him stirring a huge pot of his sauce along with a huge wooden spoon and he would ask me to "sample it."

He always had fresh Italian Bread from Uncle Mario's bakery and would dip it in the sauce and say "here Laur, taste this." It was the best sauce I ever had. We all used to say "who had the better sauce; Frankie or Nonie?" Of course, it was she who taught him the recipe, but I always insisted that his was just a little better than hers! Many of us often told him that he should market and bottle it. For one reason or another, it just never happened. It would have been a great success.

He used to tell me "the apple doesn't fall far from the tree," and that includes my tendencies to cook like him. There will be more to come regarding that! His baseball size meatballs sat in that sauce all day, and really were to die for! Cousin Alberto and I make them to this day and always think of him. I don't know about Alberto, but I know I cannot duplicate it *exactly* as Dad did but I've been trying to perfect it, as close as I can over the years!

The Blue Room was beautiful. It accommodated 80 -100 or so people, lavishly decorated in blue and gold with typical Italian flare. Big mirrors with gold painted frames, beautiful sculptures and painted pictures on the walls. Nonie had even purchased a "portable" dance floor which they set up and used when they started hiring weekend entertainment. They often had people perform for New Year's Eve celebrations. They were finally able to begin to promote private parties and functions, as well as many milestone celebrations of mine and other family members, which I cherish and will never forget.

I was very lucky growing up to have a family who owned a successful Italian Restaurant, but of course at the time, I didn't realize what I had. I can remember even as far back as grammar school when the restaurant was closed on a Tuesday, Mom and Dad threw a wonderful Halloween party for me and my friends. What fun we had bobbing for apples and running around a restaurant that was all to ourselves.

Things like my Sweet 16, Cathedral High School graduation, Elms College Graduation, as well as when I graduated from Histology training from Hartford Hospital were held in the Blue Room. My Grandparents had a lovely 50th wedding anniversary that was held there as well. Many relatives had parties there also. These were wonderful happy times in our lives.

I remember going to Ciro's before my proms at the lovely Chez Joseph banquet facility in Agawam, MA, as well as The Oaks banquet room, located in Springfield at that time. Dad wanted to take pictures with me and my date before we left for our exciting evening. Family pictures were also taken. One thing I did love was bringing my friends there to eat dinner. Cousin Alberto did the same. A lot of kids envied us at the time, and I couldn't understand why? Looking back now, I realize just what we had, and how wonderfully lucky we were.

Things were not always happy, as most people experience in life. My mother got ill, and passed away in 1980, as previously mentioned. I was just entering my first year of Cathedral High School. It was shortly after the Blue Room opened. My life crumbled in front of me. My family was devastated. Nana, my mother's mom, knew the restaurant atmosphere wasn't the best thing for a child to be exposed. Restaurant life is a hard life. Dad had so many obligations with the restaurant. My family thought it would be better for me to grow up in a more "stable" environment.

The restaurant business is very busy and there just would not have been the time to devote to bringing up a young adolescent. Nana felt so alone after Mom died and was more than willing to have me come back to live with her. It was the best thing for the both of us. Being that I was only 14 when my mother passed, Dad or various cousins would drive to Nana's house to bring us down to the restaurant for dinner and spend time with my other side of the family. When I finally was driving on my own, we would frequent the restaurant at least weekly to dine and visit with the family.

Dad always had some type of wonderful goodie or surprise to give me every time I saw him. He was great for doing that for Cousin Alberto and me. He knew many people and "peddlers" that would frequently stop in Ciro's to see what they could entice him with. He was a big kid himself, and loved seeing the look on my face when he gave me a great gadget or gift. He loved to collect all kinds of things, and if there was something I told him I'd like to have, he'd almost always have a way of pulling it out of nowhere. He always tried to obtain anything myself or Alberto wanted. We were pretty lucky kids, to say the least.

After Papa's stroke, Nonie hired a personal nurse to tend to him and help out as needed. Betty James, a wonderful woman and exceptional RN became part of our extended family. She would be present for most of our events, holidays, and almost always would be found at Nonie and Papa's house. On any given evening when Nana and I would come down to the restaurant for dinner with the family, she and Auntie Clara joined us for dinner and it was so nice.

The big "round table" in the back of the restaurant, near Nonie's office was where we always would sit to eat. Even if it was Nana and me going initially to eat alone, we would end up moving to sit with Nonie, Papa, and Betty because they were just about to have dinner. That way, we would all be together. If any extended family were there, Nonie would always insist they sit down with us too. There was always a bottle or two of wine on the table (one, always Blue Nun) and lots of fresh hot Italian bread before the meal began.

We'd always begin with a cup of the restaurant's soup of the day, which could be anything from escarole and little meatballs (polpetta) in a delicious chicken broth or tortellini or minestrone, all which were delicious and favorites. We would have a large antipasto or family style salad with black olives and anchovies, dressed with our Italian dressing to pass around.

Cousin Corrine Lattell spoke to me recently, telling me how her Dad, my Uncle Carmino would take her and her sister Darlene to Ciro's every Friday night. That was usually the night they had the pasta Fagioli on the menu. She told me how much she loved it and has said that she "never found one that quite compared to Ciro's." Corrine was kind enough to give me her recipe for it, which she said originally was her Dad's recipe and a version of Ciro's.

Cousin Carla (Stone) Sarno stated that "We always went to Ciro's for dinner as a family. It was always an awesome meal. Everyone knew everyone that was there. It felt like home."

Another one of everyone's favorite dish was called Ciro's special potatoes. They would always be served on a large oval silver platter, which I still remember to this day. The recipe was simple, but they tasted almost like a potato chip because they were so thin and delicious. Sautéed onions would be scattered around them, with a hint of salt. We all craved them, and customers craved them even more because Ciro's was the only restaurant who made them.

The main course was always different. Sometimes my grandmother wanted Fettucine Carbonara. It was a dish she loved to make, but it was not on our menu. There was always some type of pasta served with the main entrée, whether it was ziti or spaghetti always served with our homemade marinara sauce. I remember Papa always asking for the grated cheese that was on the table. I can see him "shaking away" because he loved it on his pasta, as well as the red pepper flakes that were also kept on the table.

Soon after finishing our pasta, we would order our main entree. It could have been from a juicy steak, Seafood Fra Diavolo, Chicken Marsala or Veal Parmesan. Whatever we felt like, the kitchen chefs would make for us. Those were just a few of our many wonderful dishes being served on any given night at Ciro's.

This was a perfect time for our family to gather around and talk about what was going on in our lives. Cousin Alberto and I were always asked about how school was going, or what was new with us. We all loved to gossip and have a lot of laughs. Don't get me wrong, we had our disputes also, many times right in the middle of dinner! We were like any typical Italian family. Arguing one moment, then hugging and making up the next just like it never happened! Ah, you've got to love Italian culture.

I often felt bad because Aunt Rose could never sit with us because she was so busy being the hostess and making sure things were running smoothly in the dining area and the kitchen. It was the same situation with Dad because he most often was tending to the lounge customers. Every now and then I would see him looking out through the opening of the brick wall that separated the dining area from the lounge, listening to us and watching us. He loved to interject a wise crack or comment, to make us laugh if we were talking about someone or something... Frankie was always a joker and a wise guy.

Sometimes he'd be able to sneak out for a few moments, and sit with us and then I would follow him back into the lounge or into my grandmother's office where he would ask me how my week was going, and if I needed anything. He always asked me what food I wanted to take back to my Nana's house or to the College I went to which was Our Lady of the Elms located in Chicopee, MA. It was only a five-minute ride or so to get to Nana's, but I had chosen to live in the dorms at school during the 4-year period in which I attended. So often my friends were excited when I would bring containers of food from the restaurant. It was such a treat and a break from the on-campus cafeteria food that we frequently ate. We would have a great meal once we were finished studying!

My friends often knew I was bringing food because they said they could smell the aromas of Italian food when I pulled into the parking lot! Dad made it easy putting everything in white Styrofoam containers inside cardboard boxes. After we ate, they were already asking me when I would be going to see my Dad again so I could bring all that great food for us again! The Elms even compiled a cookbook, which I still have to this day. Everyone asked me if my family would contribute some recipes from Ciro's. Nonie was thrilled and submitted a few of her favorites.

As I had mentioned previously, we always celebrated each other's birthdays. Papa's birthday was March 19th. In the Catholic faith, this day is considered a religious holiday as well. It is Saint Joseph's Day, patron Saint of the family, and was always a tradition for my Grandmother and or my Dad to make fried dough loaded with sugar. He made it in the back kitchen of the Blue Room, which I came to call "Dad's kitchen." We'd eat it as our dessert, along with my Grandfather's birthday cake!

Most, if not all of the wonderful cakes we had were from the Italian pastry bakery, La Fiorentina located directly across the street from Ciro's. On many occasions, we would order their traditional Italian rum cake, but my favorite that they made was a fresh fruit layered cake with real whipped cream, as the frosting. Let us not forget their wonderful traditional Italian cookies and cannoli that we often had. Delizioso! La Fiorentina was and still is the best Italian Bakery around, in my opinion. I have had Italian pastries and cakes from bakeries all over New England, and I have yet to find one that even comes close in authenticity and quality.

Dad`s last Christmas at
Nonie`s house, 1995

Nonie & Papa`s house
Christmas time

Me with Aunt Rose, Thanksgiving 1995

Special moment with Papa at the
Mountain Laurel Restaurant

Another special moment with
Papa at my Confirmation

Dad, Me and lovely cake at Nonie's

Thanksgiving with Dad, our last

Dad, me and Alberto during my sweet 16 party in the Blue Room

At Ciro's before Cathedral High School Senior Prom, 1984

Nonie, Nana and me enjoying dinner at Ciro's

Nonie entertaining me and my friends

Alberto and Me, Elms College
Graduation 1988

Great times, Old Ciro's

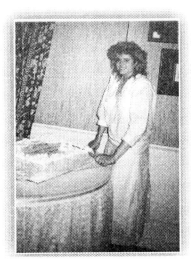

Elms College Graduation Party

Sweet 16

Me and Dad at the Elms College

Graduation from Histology School with Dad

51

Nonie and papa celebrating 50 years

Dad with Ciro`s Rams football team

New Year's Eve in lounge with
Dad`s many awards in background

52

Me and my husband John Mullin

Me and little Alberto in Nonie's
backyard mid 1970's

One of the many Our Lady of Mt
Carmel Feasts in the South End of
Springfield MA, Circa 1950's

Getting Personal: Holiday Memories and Traditions

Grandmother Rose strongly believed in the Italian tradition of a close knit family, and being together as often as possible was very important to her. This is especially typical for most Italian-Americans. I can especially agree with this today looking back, as most of my immediate family are now departed from this world, with the exception of Aunt Rose, Cousin Alberto, and his wife, Jennifer. There will always be my extended family of wonderful cousins who are all still with us also. Things are different now, as everyone has their own families with their own traditions, which makes it very difficult to connect. Still, the memories live strong in my heart and mind.

The most religious holidays that we celebrated were Easter and Christmas Eve. Thanksgiving was a huge gathering also, but entirely for the food. These were the rare times the restaurant was closed to the public, aside from the regular Tuesdays. Most of the cooking for our family holidays took place and was prepared in the back kitchen of the Blue Room. Nonie prepared many dishes in her home too, and my Dad would be at Ciro's cooking there. He loved to help her prepare all the wonderful foods we would have. He would be up for days on end, getting everything done. I remember coming to her house, the aromas lingering down the walkway to the side door where the kitchen was.

When Thanksgiving rolled around again, they'd be up all night preparing all the food. We weren't like most families, who normally just make a turkey dinner. We'd have pasta, salad, and 4 or 5 different vegetable dishes and, of course, not just Pumpkin pie but at least one Apple, Banana Cream, Chocolate Cream, and Pecan. You name it, we had it! It was wonderful.

Christmas Eve was always special. As many Italian-Americans know, the Feast of the Seven Fishes is a tradition. That evening was reserved for our immediate family. It was a quiet evening compared to all the hustle and bustle of relatives and friends coming in and out on Christmas Day. When my mother was still living, she, Nana, and I would go there early to help set the table and help my Aunt Rose set things up. Once that was done, Cousin Alberto and I usually went into the "parlor" as my Nonie called it, to watch TV and wait to be called to the table.

I used to love when they prepared Baccala (cured and salted cod fish, that is soaked in water a minimum of 2 days, changing the water every 8 hours or so). This removes all the salt from the fish so it can be cooked for consumption. Frying it was one way they prepared it, along with breading and frying Smelts. It was so delicious when it came right out of the oil.

Another wonderful dish that we had was Nonie's scungilli salad, which was served cold, and probably our most favorite, angel hair pasta with anchovy sauce and capers. I always loved when Aunt Rose would put together Finocchi (a crisp vegetable which looks like celery and tastes like Anise). It simply was cut into bite size pieces and served with a dish of olive oil, which had salt sitting on one side of the bottom of the bowl and pepper on the other. We would dip it in and enjoy every crunchy bite.

Christmas day we would be gathered back at Nonie and Papa's home for a lovely Christmas dinner. The menu was ham, turkey and roast beef along with many side dishes of various vegetables, salads, cheese plates, and antipastos. As soon as I arrived, Dad and Nonie always made sure I made a visit to all the relatives who lived in the next two houses, and upstairs from Nonie and Papa to pay respect and to visit all our Aunts, Uncles, and Cousins. It was all about family on Christmas.

Many times after the holiday season when I would stop down to give Nonie and Papa a visit, I would walk two houses down to visit Auntie Clara. I took a chance just "popping in," but she was often home and loved seeing me and having some chit chat and company. It gave us some personal time to talk. She, like Nonie, would have something on the stove simmering and always offered me something to eat.

We would talk about many things, most relating to our personal lives. I could talk to her about anything. She gave me great advice about things that were bothering me. I guess you can say she got me. We seemed to have a special connection with each other. Auntie Clara often spoke of my mom, and how much she missed her and what a lovely person she was. We'd talk about the happenings at Ciro's and later on, its unfortunate closing. Dad was always a topic that made us laugh because there were so many stories of how he was such a prankster, and as a child what Italians would call a "piccolo diablo" (little devil)! He also was a very quiet and humble man.

There were always relatives and "unexpected guests" who would show up at the door. Nonie, Papa, and Dad always insisted they sit down and eat something. It was our way. The Italian way. Spending time with relatives was most important. The gift exchanging and opening our Christmas stockings filled with unique goodies occurred after all the visitors and extended family had left. This was what my cousin and I always looked forward to especially when we were children.

It was a long couple of days, but we wouldn't have had it any other way. Aunt Rose, who is a cleaning "wiz," very neat and organized, always found room for every leftover thing that needed to be put back to its rightful place. There would be leftovers "for days" and Nonie was always very generous and made sure everyone left with something to take home.

Easter time wasn't much different. Dad and his cousin Jim Langone were very close. Every single year for Easter, they would be up all hours cooking and baking at the restaurant after it had closed for that evening. They made many of our favorite and traditional dishes which many Italian-Americans love and make themselves. Things like "Italian Macaroni Pie," Sweet ricotta pie and of course "Pizza Gaina," bread stuffed with cheeses, eggs, and usually some sort of pepperoni.

One of my favorite desserts was a simple cake that was baked in a mold of a lamb, or "Torta di Agnello." It was such a beautiful sight when it sat in the middle of the table at dessert time. It almost looked real by the way it was so beautifully frosted, sprinkled with shredded coconut around the bottom of it. It was perfect with a cup of coffee or espresso.

As Time Went On...

As I grew older, I could actually understand what it took to make a restaurant business such as Ciro's so successful. Alberto and I wish we had kept it going today. It was countless hours given by devoted people having no time off and basically working in a 24x7 hour type of business. It was important to keep reliable staff on hand and available beginning with the waitresses and busboys, dish washers, as well as experienced chefs in the kitchen. Everyone was important to some capacity or Ciro's would not be able to run the way it did for so many years. It was important to have good, strong relationships with the food and beverage vendors assuring they would deliver the freshest produce, meats, and seafood for the week.

In terms of the "front of the house" as those in the restaurant business refer, it was imperative that reservations were in place, tables were set with flatware and glasses, everything managed well down to the most finite details like making sure the salt and pepper shakers were filled, and clean linens were set. It seems insignificant but it was done not only to keep business moving at a steady pace and being able to turn tables for revenue, but also so the patrons did not have to wait too long.

We knew as time went on, it was a necessity to come up with inventive and unique specials and "events" such as adult Halloween parties, where many employees would dress up for instance. We needed to find new ways to try to draw in new business to increase revenue.

Like in life, there were minor problems which arose that affected the flow of business. That was something that my family dreaded, especially on a busy Friday or Saturday evening. Workers would call in sick or not come in for personal reasons, which really made it difficult for Ciro's to run successfully. The worst was when they would call in 15 minutes before they were due to arrive for their shift. It caused much chaos and my family would be very upset, but somehow they always seemed to find a way to pull through. Sometimes Nonie, even when she was at a point where she no longer was able stand on her legs for a long period of time, would have to make the effort to go into the kitchen to prepare whatever needed to be done.

My family was very understanding. Many of these workers should not have been able to return because of their history of not showing up or constantly calling in. But my family would always put their hands out and give them a second chance. It was their generosity that made them the wonderful people that they were (and those of us that are left still are). It's just something inbred in us.

Dad would always be willing to help out the local vagrants that came by, either by giving them something to eat, or giving them some money to try to help them get back on their feet. These qualities were wonderful, but I know many people took advantage of my family because of their tremendous generosity and trust in people. This, in my opinion was one of the main factors which contributed to the demise and eventual closing of Ciro's.

The restaurant survived through the 1980s and was still going strong, especially with the private parties and events in the Blue (banquet) room, but by end of the decade, big problems began to arise. Attitudes and desires to keep Ciro's operating started to diminish. The surrounding neighborhood of the South End began to deteriorate, and as business started to decline, Nonie was faced with financial problems. Not being able to pay bills along with the increasing unreliability of the staff really took a toll.

After long and hard consideration and discussion, we realized that filing bankruptcy was the only answer. In the early 1990s, the doors of Ciro's Restaurant closed forever. We were all devastated,

Dad, Nonie, and Papa along with Aunt Rose felt the huge wave of depression and darkness fall upon them. What they had loved, lived for and worked so hard for to be successful had to finally come to an end. Heartbroken would be the best word to describe the feelings we all had, extended family included. It was something they never got over.

Nonie and Papa always kept a glimmer of hope, and they wished for the restaurant to be able to be turned around and brought back to life. Unfortunately, this never happened. They both had been taken ill physically, and Dad had done all he could do. As many contacts and friends that he had who wanted to help him, for one reason or another just couldn't do it. Without the capital to get Ciro's back to opening its doors, it just couldn't happen. It was an end of an era that would not soon be forgotten.

Nonie, Papa, Aunt Rose and of course myself, never expected Dad to pass away before everyone's eyes at the very young age of 52. None of the family did. I knew to some capacity, we were still holding onto the dream, hoping that he would help bring the beloved Ciro's back. Memories haunt me still when I think of the phone ringing at 3am, and Cousin Jim Langone telling me what had happened to Dad. He had a massive heart attack while helping the family clear snow during the blizzard of January

9th, 1996. It also was his birthday that day which made things even harder for us. This couldn't be happening, but it was real, very surreal.

Although very different circumstances when I lost Mom at such a young age, I still had the same exact feeling inside thinking it wasn't true. I wanted to believe that it was just a bad nightmare, but it wasn't. A piece of my heart will always remain broken, for losing two of the most important people in my life. Shortly thereafter and all within 1 year, we lost Nonie, then Papa. Nana had passed a few years previous in 1993. I think because of these tragedies in our lives, it has made us stronger people in ways which I cannot explain.

Before Dad passed, I used to call him frequently. I had moved up to South Deerfield, MA, in the early 1990s. It's about an hour drive to Springfield, so I didn't see the family as much as I was able to previously. My first husband Jim was originally from South Deerfield, so I made the decision to move up there with him. Luckily the phone was never far away and if I wanted to cook something and just couldn't remember exactly how Dad or Nonie had made it, I'd just give them a call. We never wrote any of our recipes down, it was all in our heads and our hearts! He would tell me exactly what I needed for ingredients and go over the recipe and instructions step by step.

The last memory I have speaking to Dad was actually the morning that he passed away during that blizzard. I had called to wish him a Happy Birthday. We chatted, then the last thing he said to me was "Lauren, be careful and watch yourself (he always said that to me) and don't go out if you don't need to. I love you." In response I said, "No Dad, YOU be careful, love you too and talk with you soon." Those words haunt me to this day. I vividly remember standing by the wall phone, where Jim and I were living in South Deerfield. I was looking out the window watching the snow come down and seeing the storm intensify very quickly before my eyes.

After his passing, Nonie was great for helping me too. I remember going to her house one particular day, and she taught me about the different shrimp sizes they use in the restaurant business. We sat down, and she then proceeded to show me how to clean (devein) the shrimp properly and how to clean mushrooms. Finally, she showed me how she made the stuffing for them.

I was anxious and just wanted to start cooking! She always told me to take my time, and make sure everything was right. Cooking comes from the heart, and you must love what you're doing. That is the secret she told me. It's "the love." Finally, we stuffed our shrimp and mushrooms and baked them.

I can still smell the aroma in her kitchen of all the garlic. It's a lovely memory that I will never forget.

Cousin John Grondalski recalls when he was asked to help make stuffed artichokes. What a wonderful recipe that is and one that was always on the Ciro's menu. All of us kids have always been involved with food, whether eating it or making it! And I know I can speak for all of us, we are grateful for our families teaching us what we know and love to do today.

.

Final Thoughts...

Myself and my family included have made an attempt to carry on with our lives, some days more difficult than others, but we know our loved ones look down upon us and are by our side every step we take, every day. If nothing else, they are close in our hearts and minds. Our Italian-American roots run deep, and our ties have always been strong, no matter what difficulty or tragedy we have had to endure. This is something that Nonie always believed in. It's something we grew up with.

The best thing and only thing I have left are memories. These memories are so vivid and strong in my mind and heart and linger to this day. I'm sure I can speak for our remaining and extended family, whom I'm sure feel the same way. Every time I drive by our old restaurant, I have such bittersweet memories because I miss it so very much and wish things were the way they used to be.

I have looked at our old parking lot, adjacent to Ciro's building which still stands there today. But it is not just a parking lot to me. It's filled with so many memories, like seeing Dad during the Our Lady of Mt. Carmel Feast. He would be cooking Italian sausages with peppers and onions that could be smelt a block away. He had such a happy and content look on his face. Adjacent to where he was set up to cook, there was a tent with tables and chairs for people to sit and enjoy.

I recently spoke to a good friend of his, Anthony Manzi, owner of Music Tribute Productions, a booking agency and DJ service who told me, "During the Feast, in front of Ciro's your dad used to have a hand gun that would shoot fireworks in the air!" That must have been a sight to see, and definitely a typical thing my dad would do to amuse people! Anthony is from Springfield, and told me he would often order "food to go." One of his personal favorites was Ciro's famous cold broccoli and the baked rigatoni with ricotta and mozzarella.

I have memories of Dad walking me out to my car with containers of his wonderful sauce and food that was prepared, seeing him bent over to put them in the trunk. Memories of when I would look at Mt. Carmel School and Church where I attended, thinking of the many school and church events of which we were a part of. I see us walking through that parking lot across the street to La Fiorentina bakery for cannoli and pastry or walking just a few doors down into Uncle Mario's Italian bakery for bread.

I definitely will not forget the times we would walk from Ciro's over to Albano's market, which was on East Columbus Avenue for the best Italian lemon ice, and stopping in at Frigo's market, just around the corner on William Street if we felt like making a nice Italian grinder with their wonderful cold cuts and cheeses. Milano Market was a place we also frequented. Let us not forget Mom & Rico's specialty market. Rico Daniele, the owner, was another personal friend to my Dad. His business located diagonally across the street from Ciro's.

If you travel north down Main Street not too far from Ciro's, you will see the Iconic Red Rose Pizzeria. They serve the most authentic and delicious pizza for miles! Then if you walk south on Main (actually the next block over from Ciro's) was our Cousin Frank Langone's florist. They provided many beautiful arrangements over the years for our family. It was Langone's florist who arranged all the beautiful flowers and bridal bouquet for my first wedding.

One thing about the South End of Springfield when Ciro's was open was the fact that everyone supported and shopped at local markets and businesses. The South End had become a very close knit Italian community. That type of thing, in my opinion, is almost impossible to find in today's world. Modern ways and greed to succeed have many businesses only looking out for themselves. Many don't even know what businesses reside adjacent or across the street from them, and they don't seem to care.

These are some of the reasons I feel the need to tell my story, my life, growing up in and around an Italian Restaurant and to stress how important and proud I am to be an Italian-American. I have been left with so many traditions and things which I have learned and observed over the years. I feel so lucky to have been taught these values and traditions.

I am able to share them with the wonderful man I met and married, John Mullin. After my first husband Jim and I divorced, I moved back to the Springfield area and spent a lot of time with Aunt Rose. It was good for the both of us to be there for one another. When I met John, I knew he was the man I wanted to be with for the rest of my life, so I decided to move to his hometown of Worcester, MA, where I currently reside with him. His family and grown children are also there. That is why I made the decision to leave Springfield, once again.

I hope that all my remaining relatives, friends, and of course the patrons of the former, the original, the one and only Ciro's of the South End of Springfield, Massachusetts read, connect, and enjoy what I have presented here. Anyone can name their business Ciro's. In fact, it's a very popular restaurant name seen across the country, but no one can or ever will duplicate the traditions, the atmosphere, the people, and the original recipes that my family created over the years that made Ciro's special and such a success. Most importantly, it is the memories that people remember, made,, and associate with the Ciro's Restaurant, they knew and loved for so many years.

An Italian-American couple living in the South End of Springfield had the American dream to purchase their own business and make a contribution to the community while making it a success for themselves and their family. That couple, Albert and Rose Scibelli, made that happen. A lot of blood, sweat, and tears made it happened. I'm proud to have had the privilege of being taught the meaning of tradition and the importance of what having good values and work ethic mean while growing up in and around our restaurant…. Ciro's Restaurant.

FAMILY

RECIPES

APPETIZERS

Some of these dishes were served at Ciro's,
some we made for our own family and special
occasions or at various times of the year. All
are delicious! Mangia Bene!

Frankie's Sausage, Peppers, and Onion Grinders

Not really an "appetizer," but for us, it could be. I see Dad at the flat top grill during the Italian Feast, doing what he loved the most, cooking! He always used nice sweet pork Italian sausage and bell peppers sliced in strips and onions that were caramelized and smelled so sweet.

2-3 lbs. sweet pork Italian Sausages

2-3 bell peppers, red and or green

3-4 large sweet onions

Salt, pepper, garlic powder, and olive oil

12 fresh Italian grinder rolls

Pour about a cup or so of water into a sauté pan, then add the sausages and cover so they can cook. Once this is done drain water and add a few tablespoons of olive oil into a large sauté pan. Add the sausages back in and let them simmer until brown on all sides.

In a separate large sauté pan, add olive oil to coat the bottom, and add uniformly sliced bell peppers and sliced onions. Add Salt and Pepper and some garlic, if you like for added flavor.

Let cook until peppers are tender and onions are caramelized, approximately 10-15 minutes.

While everything is still warm, begin to assemble the Italian grinder rolls and stuff each one with above ingredients. If you like, you can slice the sausage lengthwise before adding the peppers and onions.

Ciro's famous Cold Broccoli

Mom made this when she worked the salad station in the kitchen at Ciro's. It's a very easy dish to make, but all the clientele and even the employees raved about how wonderful this cold appetizer was. Aunt Rose also made this dish, and it was just as good. She and Mom had a special "touch" and were able to make something so simple, taste so wonderful.

3 bunches broccoli

2 fresh lemons. (One for juice and one for wedges on the platter)

Olive oil

Salt, pepper, and garlic to taste

Cut the hard stalk ends off the broccoli, but leave some for "presentation." Add them to a pot of boiling water to blanch for approximately 5 minutes or until bright green.

Remove and shock in cold ice water to prevent further cooking. (The broccoli should be firm, yet fork tender.) Cut the large pieces lengthwise, and place on a platter. Squeeze the juice of ½ a lemon over it and drizzle extra virgin olive oil. Add salt, pepper, and garlic to taste.

Serve with cut lemon wedges along the side of the platter.

If you use spinach, you can steam it down in a pan with a lid on it, about 4-5 minutes. Remember, it may look like a lot, but it cooks way down! Let it cool, then add a drizzle of olive oil, and a pinch of garlic, salt, and pepper. Don't forget your lemon and wedges.

Shrimp a la Ciro

This is a classic Ciro's appetizer and another one that Ciro's clientele love. I love it too! We would usually make it in the summer months because it's served cold and the lemon makes it so fresh tasting!

1 pound cooked shrimp cleaned and deveined

3 ribs of celery

1 can black pitted olives

1 small red onion

3-4 ripe tomatoes

Fresh bunch of parsley

Extra virgin olive oil

2 lemons

Salt, pepper & garlic powder

Clean and cook the shrimp. Size here doesn't matter because it will be diced with all the other ingredients. Once cooked, let cool and drain on paper towel. Dice all the above ingredients, small and as uniformly as possible.

Now cooled, add the shrimp into a large serving bowl. Toss with the fresh chopped parsley, olive oil, juice of both lemons (taste it at this point, you may only want or need to add 1 lemon, depending on your liking). Add salt, pepper, and garlic to taste as well.

Let it sit for a while, so all the flavors meld together. Serve cold with additional lemon wedges.

Classic Italian Antipasto

There are many variations to this dish, but this is the way I remember it always being made at Ciro's. Never any lettuce!!

¼ lb. genoa salami, sliced thin

¼ lb. mortadella

1/4lb thinly sliced prosciutto

1/4lb each sweet and hot capicola

½ lb. sharp sliced provolone

6-8 anchovy fillets

A handful of pepperoncini and olives (black or green)

2 sliced hard boiled eggs

6-8 roasted and marinated roasted red pepper slices

½ cup marinated mushrooms

8-10 radishes and sliced purple onion for garnish

We used to roll the meat and cheese by cutting a slit from the middle to the end so you could lift and tuck it almost like a funnel. To make it look like a pretty flower you can either put a carved radish or a black or green olive in the center. Garnish along the platter with the onions and place all the other ingredients however you like on a large platter to make it pretty!

Melon and Prosciutto

This was a popular dish, especially in the summer months when it was hot, and the melon was cold and refreshing. A simple dish, yet at very popular one at Ciro's back in the day.

½ of a cold honeydew melon cut into thin wedges

¼ lb. paper thin prosciutto

The secret here is that the melon should be at its peak of ripeness and so very sweet, then gently wrap the thinly sliced prosciutto around it from one end of the melon to the other. Serve on a nice platter.

Insalata Caprese (Fresh Tomato, Basil, and Mozzarella Cheese)

This is such a classic recipe and so very easy. The only reason I put this one in this book is because it invokes memories of me seeing my Dad, on a warm summer day picking his oh so very ripe tomatoes off the plants he had growing in large pots in and around Nonie's backyard, as well as the fresh basil he had growing as well.

1-2 big juicy ripe red tomatoes cut very thick

1 ball of fresh thickly cut pieces of mozzarella cheese

A handful fresh basil, straight from the plant, if possible

Extra virgin olive oil, salt and pepper

Arrange your slices of tomato and cheese on a platter, and gently tear the basil into pieces and place all over the platter, drizzle olive oil, and add a fair amount of salt and pepper.
Sometimes he would add a few slices of purple onion to the dish as well.

Stuffed Artichokes

This was a very popular recipe on the appetizer portion of the menu at Ciro's, as well as one my cousin John Grondalski's favorites. I thank him for his contribution of his version of this classic recipe and memories that go along with it. He tells me how he recalls learning how to make these as a little boy at his Grandmother's home (one of my Grandfather's sisters) who lived on the top floor of their 2 family home on Fremont Street in the South End of Springfield.

4-6 raw artichokes

1 cup of seasoned bread crumbs

1 cup of grated parmesan cheese

1/3 cup olive oil

4 cups of chicken stock

4-6 garlic cloves

Cut the stems off the bottom of each artichoke so they sit flat in a 3-4" deep baking dish.

Clip off the pointy tip of each leaf. This part is a bit time consuming, but well worth the effort.

Fluff to open up the leaves of the artichoke.

In a bowl, mix the seasoned breadcrumbs, grated cheese, and enough olive oil so the mixture is wet and slightly sticks together, but not runny. Beginning at the bottom of each leaf on the artichoke add the mixture with a spoon (or your hands) in between each leaf and work your way to the top.

Once all the artichokes are stuffed, use a grate so they are not sitting directly on the bottom of the dish and gently pour the chicken stock in, placing the garlic in and around the broth as well. Make sure the broth is up to the base of the artichoke and drizzle olive oil over the top of them.

Place them in an oven preheated to 350 degrees until you see that the leaves are steamed enough and begin to pull away from the core. Monitor the liquid level and if necessary add more stock, so the dish does not dry out on the bottom.

Clams Casino

Coming from a restaurant family, Alberto and I were lucky to try and enjoy an amazing variety of food. This was not only from our family but from others that Nonie and Papa knew. Because of that, we have such developed palates. We are very grateful for that. Not many little children would like (or even try) something like clams casino!

2 dozen little neck clams

1 red or yellow bell pepper

6 slices of bacon

½ cup melted butter

½ cup dry white wine

1/3 Italian seasoned bread crumbs

1 fresh lemon

1 small bunch of parsley chopped

2-3 cloves of garlic chopped

These clams must be soaked to remove any sand, and then shucked with a very sharp edge knife. Make sure you reserve any juice from the clams for later. Roast, peel, and dice the peppers. Top each clam with a few pieces of pepper, and a few pieces of bacon that has also been "diced" into small pieces.

Proceed with placing a drizzle of butter onto each clam, then add wine, fresh chopped parsley all mixed together with the bread crumbs. Add the remainder of the melted butter over each clam and nestle in a baking dish. The oven should be preheated to 450 degrees. Once it is to the right temperature, bake the "stuffing" until it is brown and the bacon ever so crisp (about 10-12 minutes). Put under the broiler for the last minute or so to ensure everything is brown.

Once on a serving platter, gently pour the reserved clam "juice" and the juice from a few wedges of lemon.

Escargot (land snails) in Garlic Butter Sauce

I was a very little girl when I first experienced escargot. One evening as we all sat for dinner at Ciro's, Dad had escargot brought out for me to try! I still remember the look on my Mother and Nana's face because they couldn't believe that I loved these little delicacies. Dad showed me the "proper" way to eat them, using a spoon shaped tong to grip the shells they were in. You gently pull them from the shell with a cocktail fork.

If you have not had the pleasure of trying these, they have a rich, buttery flavor and when loaded with melted butter, garlic, and parsley, they are so delicious. We had metal platters with indentations in them made especially for the escargot to sit in, so all that buttery garlic goodness was left, to be sopped up with a slice of fresh Italian bread.

24 snails (purchased separately from their shells)

1 thinly sliced shallot

½ cup white wine

1 whole head of garlic, peeled and chopped

1 ounce of flat leaf parsley chopped

1 stick of butter, melted

Salt and pepper

Italian bread (served on the side)

In a sauté pan, combine the snails, shallot, and white wine and bring to simmer. Cook for 15 minutes or so, and then set the snails aside. Combine finely chopped garlic and parsley and add the butter. Mix until spreadable. Season with salt and pepper.

Take snail shells and place a snail in each, then stuff remaining space inside with the garlic-parsley butter. Once this is done, simply preheat the oven to broil, place snails in a baking dish, or if you have a platter designed specifically for escargot and broil until the butter is sizzling. Serve immediately with fresh sliced Italian bread.

Pasta Fagioli

Cousin Corrine Lattell gave me her recipe for this wonderful soup! She tells me it was a version of Ciro's, and remembers when her Dad (my Uncle Carmino) used to take her and her sister Darlene every Friday night to Ciro's for dinner. That was the night Ciro's used to have pasta fagioli on the menu. She said and I quote "I loved Ciro's Pasta Fagioli and out of every restaurant I've been to since then, nothing comes close other than the recipe my father made at home. It's even better the next day!"

2 tbsp. olive oil

1 one clove garlic (crushed)

Half/slab salt pork cut into chunks

3 stalks chopped celery (with leaves)

4 small cans of chicken broth

3 small cans of water, using the chicken broth cans

1 small can of tomato paste

1 box of ditalini pasta

1 can of small white beans

Chopped parsley

Heat 2 tbsp. olive oil with crushed garlic, salt pork and celery in a large stock pot. Simmer ingredients until salt pork and celery get soft (about 5 minutes). Add the chicken broth and water to the pot with the tomato paste (use about ¾ of the can). Let this come to a boil, and then reduce heat to simmer for 90 minutes. Toward the end, add the ditalini and cook until al dente. Also, add the beans (juice and all) and simmer for 5 minutes. Let sit for 15-30 minutes before serving. The first day will be more "soup" consistency, while the next day will be more of a pasta dish (you can thin with water or chicken stock if you want it soupier). Serve sprinkled with chopped parsley and grated cheese (optional).

Manest (Escarole and beans)

Walking on Fremont Street to visit Nonie, I could smell the aromas on the stove as she was simmering a dish we loved, called Manest. She and Papa were just getting ready to sit down to eat lunch, so of course I joined them.

2-3 bunches escarole (rinsed very well and chopped)

2-3 large 48oz cans of white beans

1 cup pepperoni cut in chunks

3-4 quarts chicken stock

3 tbsp.p olive oil

4 cloves chopped garlic

Ham bone for flavor

Grated parmesan cheese

1 loaf of Italian bread

Rinse off the heads of escarole to ensure there is no sandy grit trapped in the leaves. Cut into small pieces. In a large stock pot add the oil, garlic, and the escarole and begin to "sauté."

Add the chunks of pepperoni, the cannellini (white) beans in their juice, and the chicken stock. For added flavor, you can add a ham bone which will add a nice smoky flavor to the Manest. Remove the bone, just before serving.

Once all the escarole has wilted down and the flavors have melded (the longer the better), serve in a nice bowl. Top with some additional olive oil if you wish and grated parmesan cheese to taste. It will get thicker by the next day. Grab a hunk of Italian bread to go with it. We used to love it that way. If you want more of a soupy consistency, just add a bit more chicken stock.

Side Dishes

Fresh Green Beans in Tomato Sauce

Most Italian-Americans I know love this dish. When the green beans are at their peak of freshness during the summer months and they are added to fresh tomatoes to make a quick red sauce, it's a marriage made in heaven!

1-2 lbs. fresh whole green beans

3-4 cloves garlic minced

½ cup olive oil

Salt, pepper

Handful of fresh basil leaves, torn in pieces

2-3 cups of Italian canned peeled tomatoes, with juice or your favorite red sauce

Clean both ends of (string) beans, and blanch in a pot of salted boiling water for 3-4 minutes. Drain water and shock beans in a bowl with ice and water to prevent from cooking further. The beans should be tender, not soggy.

In a large skillet, add olive oil and garlic and let begin to cook, 2-3 minutes. Break up the whole tomatoes with your hands over the skillet, and let all the juices fall into the pan as well. Simmer for 10 minutes.

Add the green beans, salt, and pepper into the skillet with the tomato "sauce." Continue to cook for 5 minutes or so. Add fresh basil.

Transfer to a large bowl and serve family style with your entrée of choice.

Italian Potato Salad

One of our family's personal favorites. I still make it to this day, especially on a hot summer day, for a bbq or party. I remember having this on Father's Day and on the 4th of July at Nonie's house. My Aunt Rose is great at making this!

5 lb. bag of cooked, diced potatoes. (Preferably red skin potatoes, leave the skin on)

1 large purple onion

1 can pitted black olives

5 stalks chopped celery

Fresh chopped parsley

Fresh garlic, salt and pepper

1 lemon, freshly squeezed

½ cup or more extra virgin olive oil.

Chop all ingredients, aside from the potatoes, which should be fork tender and cut into bite size pieces. Mix all ingredients while potatoes are still lukewarm (room temperature). Add oil cover and chill. Before serving, gently mix all ingredients, taste, and see if more oil is needed. As the ingredients meld together, the oil soaks in, so more may be needed before putting in large serving bowl. It is best to set for anywhere from a few hours to overnight.

Jambota

This is a lovely summer dish because it's best when all the vegetables are fresh and in season. Nonie used to make this one at home for us, and we all enjoyed it.

2 medium eggplants

2 each green, yellow and red peppers

2 medium zucchinis

2 small yellow squash

4-5 potatoes

1 large onion

2-3 cloves of garlic

Olive oil, salt and pepper

Cut and dice into chunk size pieces all the above vegetables. In one pan add olive oil and a clove of minced garlic and fry the potatoes by themselves. In another pan add the olive oil and remaining garlic and sauté all the other chunks of cut vegetables, making sure to seed the peppers until tender.

Preheat oven to 400 degrees, arrange your cut, fried potatoes on the bottom of the baking dish then add all the other sautéed vegetables on top of the browned potatoes. Add salt, pepper, and a drizzle more olive oil. Bake 12-15 minutes until thoroughly cooked.

Stuffed Mushrooms

Stuffed mushrooms were a Ciro's favorite. I remember Nonie showing me how to take the stem off the mushroom cap ever so carefully, teaching me how to make the most delicious stuffing for them. She always loved to use the very large caps.

24 jumbo white button mushrooms

3-4 cloves garlic

1 red pepper finely diced

½ cup seasoned Italian bread crumb

1/3 cup grated parmesan cheese

Bunch fresh parsley finely chopped

Olive oil, salt & pepper

½ cup chicken stock

1 cup melted butter

1 cup dry white wine

Preheat oven to 425 degrees. Once stems are carefully removed from the mushroom cap, chop them into small pieces and set aside while you seed and clean the red pepper, then chop the garlic. All pieces should be uniform in size.

In a frying pan add some olive oil and gently sauté the mushroom stems, red chopped pepper, and garlic until cooked. Once cooled, add in a bowl the bread crumbs, grated cheese, chopped fresh parsley, a dash of salt and pepper and then to that mixture add the cooked ingredients. Add a drizzle of melted butter, a small amount of chicken stock for flavor, and white wine to the whole mixture, so it becomes very moist.

Take a small amount, enough to fill each cavity of the mushroom. Butter a baking dish and line the caps one by one. Once completed, pour the remainder of wine and melted butter over and in the baking dish before putting in the oven. Bake 25 minutes or until the stuffing becomes nice and brown.

Transfer to a nice platter and serve family style for all to enjoy.

Caponata

Nonie and Dad loved to make this recipe. They usually made it in the summertime because it's when the eggplant and zucchini are at its peak of freshness. Our recipe is quite simple. I've seen very "elaborate" ones with added raisins and fennel. Our's is simple and had a resemblance to Ratatouille. It really varies from family to family.

2-3 medium eggplants

3 ribs of celery

2-3 medium zucchini

3-4 carrots

½ cup of olives

1 large onion

1 large green pepper

1-2 cups of Marinara sauce

Olive oil, salt and pepper

Add some olive oil to the pan. Cut all your vegetables into uniform chunks and pieces.

Sauté in oil until softened. Add salt and pepper. Once this is done, remove from heat, let cool a bit and add the chopped olives, marinara sauce and either serve warm or at room temperature.

Antipasto Pasta Salad

This recipe is perfect for a cookout or family gathering. We made it year round because it's so easy and flavorful. We all enjoy this one very much and it's a definite "crowd pleaser."

1 (12 ounce) box spiral macaroni (or whichever kind you like)

1 cup chopped red, green, and yellow peppers

1 ¼ cups of pitted ripe olives, sliced (you can use black or green)

½ lb. of hard salami cut into thin strips

1 small red onion cut into rings

½ cup fresh chopped parsley

¼-1/3 cup grated parmesan cheese

¾ cup of Italian dressing

Cook the pasta according to package directions. Rinse with cold water until completely cool. In a large bowl combine all the above ingredients to the pasta and toss. Let set and chill, if possible a couple hours before serving.

Aunt Rose Marconi's "famous" Bleu Cheese Dressing

My Aunt Rose Marconi has always made this incredible bleu cheese dressing. It's so cool, creamy, and tangy! I remember her giving me a quart container of it to take home with me.

1 lb. chunk bleu cheese

2 containers mayonnaise

2 containers sour cream

A good dash garlic powder

Dash of white pepper

1 tbsp. yellow mustard

¼ cup white vinegar

3 tbsp. soy sauce

Salt

Begin by crumbling the bleu cheese into the size pieces you would like in this dressing. If you want to make a couple quart size containers, add 2 jars of mayonnaise and 2 containers of sour cream in a bowl to the chunks of bleu cheese. Add in the yellow mustard, white vinegar for a nice tanginess, the soy sauce (the "secret" ingredient you would never think to put in this!) and mix very well. Add salt to taste.

Auntie Clara Fragomeni's Homemade Red Sauce

My cousin Sandy Fragomini was kind enough to give me her mom's recipe for her homemade sauce that she loved to make. Sandy says the pasta she usually had with it was ziti. You can use any kind of pasta or spaghetti you prefer. I remember enjoying her sauce when I would stop by for a visit or during the holidays. She, like Nonie, would have all kinds of food on her table for all of us to enjoy.

1 larger white onion

2 tbsp. olive oil

3-4 beef short ribs

1 can of tomato paste

1 can of crushed tomatoes

Salt to taste

A "secret" pinch of sugar

Finely chop the onion and sauté in olive oil until translucent. Put in a decent size sauce pot. To the same pan you sautéed the onions, add the short ribs and cook until browned on all sides. Put them into the sauce pot with the onion; add a small can of tomato paste and a large can of crushed tomatoes. Sandy says "the secret" is a pinch of sugar. Let simmer for an hour or so stirring occasionally. Eventually, the meat will fall off the bone, and you can fork shred it, if it hasn't done it itself already! Boil your favorite ziti or spaghetti and enjoy!

Italian Macaroni Pie

An Easter specialty, but it of course can be made anytime of the year. I remember Dad and Nonie staying up all night making this. If Nonie wasn't helping him, our cousin Jim Langone would be there to help because there was so many to make! Dad and Jim were very close cousins also! We always ate it cold straight from the refrigerator or at room temperature. Dad would say to me "Laur, just cut a square and help yourself." This particular recipe is my cousins Al and Anthony Lattell's version.

2 32 ounce containers of ricotta cheese

10 ounces of Parmigiano-Reggiano cheese

12-16 ounces shredded mozzarella cheese

12 eggs

Ground black pepper or peppercorns

2 lbs. of Perciatelli or Buccotini pasta

Pre cook the pasta, and then mix all of the ingredients together and put into a baking dish. Bake at 350 degrees for 40-45 minutes or until set and golden brown on top. Let cool, then cut into pieces and serve.

Frankie's Tennis Ball size Meatballs

One of my fondest memories when I was visiting my Dad at Ciro's was his tennis ball size meatballs. I'm not kidding about the size! I can still see him standing over the back kitchen stove of the restaurant frying them in a huge pan. Those alone, with a piece of fresh Italian bread and his "famous" marinara sauce to dip it in (more to come regarding that!) was all you would need. I know my family can still attest to that. We miss the meatballs, but we miss him more. It's not so much his meatball recipe per se, although they always had that "special" flavor and taste that no one could quite duplicate.

3-4 lbs. ground beef (80/20)

1-2 lb. ground pork

1-2 lb. ground veal

½ loaf day old Italian bread broken into small pieces

1 cup milk

3-4 beaten eggs

½ cup Italian seasoning

½ bunch fresh finely chopped parsley

3-4 finely chopped cloves of garlic

1½ cup grated parmesan cheese

Fresh chopped parsley

Good pinch of salt and black pepper

Soak the bread in milk until absorbed and squeeze out any excess, and break into little pieces. Mix with all the other above ingredients. DO NOT overwork the mixture or you will end up with very tight, tough balls. You can form the meatballs into any size you like, and fry them in a good amount of olive oil until they are browned on all sides. Achieving the "crunchy" brown outside and the soft moist flavorful inside was one of his secrets. He NEVER baked them in the oven. You can serve them, as I said, by themselves hot out of the oil once drained, or put them in your favorite sauce. He always had his huge stock pot of sauce simmering close by!

Cousin Alberto's Baccala Salad

Most Italian-Americans certainly will know and (hopefully) love Baccala (salted cod fish). Our family always had this dish during the Feast of the Seven Fishes at Christmas Eve dinner. This is how Alberto makes it. Even if it's not Christmas time, it still a very delicious "salad" and can be eaten as an entrée with some fresh Italian bread.

4-5 lbs. salt cod

Olive oil

4 stalks celery

1 can black olives

2 lemons

Salt & pepper

¼ cup capers

This recipe is a labor of love. You must soak the salt cod for 3 days, changing the water at least once a day. Chop into bite size pieces the celery, olives, and once the cod fish has been soaked thoroughly, boil it with some lemon in the water until the fish becomes tender. Once out of the water and cooled enough to handle it, break the fish with your hands into pieces. Mix all ingredients together with enough olive oil to coat, the juice of 1 lemon, and finally add the capers. Add salt and pepper to taste. Be sure to toss well and let sit refrigerated for a few hours so all the ingredients marry together. Serve with additional lemon wedges.

Cousin Carla (Stone) Sarno's version of Meatballs

If you're Italian, most people have a meatball recipe that is unique to them or one which has been passed down from their previous relatives. This is Carla's version. She calls this a "small batch."

1½ lbs. 80% ground beef

1 lb. ground pork

½ loaf Italian bread (day old)

3 cups grated Pecorino Romano

4 eggs

1 small onion

3 garlic cloves

2 tablespoons salt

4 tablespoons black pepper

1 tablespoon of red crushed pepper (she put it in by "accident" and everyone loved the "mistake")

Handful of fresh basil

Handful of fresh parsley

Olive oil

Take the bread and soak in some water. Squeeze out the excess water, and put in mixing bowl.

In that same bowl, add grated fresh onion, so it's almost liquefied. Grate in 3 cloves of fresh garlic. Add the grated pecorino, salt, pepper, and 2 eggs. Mix well.

After the bread mixture is mixed, add the beef and pork, then the rest of the ingredients, red pepper flakes and remaining 2 eggs. Chop basil and parsley and mix everything together.

Using a nonstick frying pan add olive oil so it is approximately ½ inch deep in the frying pan. Make sure the oil is hot! Start rolling the meatballs and get frying!

Entrées

Beef Rollatini (Braciola)

This dish was always a very special one to me. When Dad decided to make this, he would call me and tell me to swing by and pick up some for dinner. We always used to joke about being careful not to "choke on the toothpicks" that held them together, but most of the time he would use butcher's string to keep them in their classic rolled up shape.

2 lbs. thinly sliced (1/2 inch thick) sirloin or top round steak

3 crumbled hard boiled eggs (which are optional)

½ lb. of salt pork, ground very fine

2 cloves garlic finely chopped

½ cup finely chopped parsley

1 cup fine seasoned breadcrumbs

1 cup Romano cheese

6 thin slices proscuito

Salt and pepper

Olive oil for frying

¾ cup shredded mozzarella cheese

Spread the above ingredients in layers on the thin slices of beef and roll. Secure with toothpicks or butcher's string. Sauté in a small amount of oil until brown. Place in the oven and bake at 350 degrees for 45 minutes or until done. Cool slightly. Slice into ½ inch slices. Serve on a warm plate with spaghetti sauce or they can be served plain.

Baked Jumbo Shrimp

This recipe was served at Ciro's and was one of their most popular ones. It also has very special memories for me. I remember asking Nonie if she would teach me how to make this recipe just like she did. She loved that we had some personal time together while we sat at her kitchen table. She taught me step by step how to clean (de-vein), stuff, and bake them. She loved teaching her family these recipes that would eventually become our traditions. She always advised to get the biggest shrimp (U10s) and told me to leave the very end of the tail with the shell on so they didn't dry out when you baked them.

3-4 cloves garlic

½ cup seasoned Italian bread crumb

1/3 cup grated parmesan cheese

Bunch fresh parsley finely chopped

Olive oil, salt & pepper

½ cup chicken stock

Juice of 1 lemon

121

1 cup melted butter

1 cup dry white wine

½ red bell pepper chopped fine (optional)

Once you peel the shrimp (except the tip of the tail) and remove the "vein" along the back side of the shrimp, you must "butterfly" or gently cut the front side of the shrimp, being careful not to cut through it, so you can stuff it. After mixing all the above ingredients, use a fairly deep baking dish, as you want to put some leftover chicken stock on the bottom to keep everything moist. Stand each shrimp side by side and bake in oven at 350 degrees for 15 minutes. The last 5 minutes you can put them under the broiler to brown the lovely buttery bread crumb mixture. If you like serve on platter with lemon wedges and additional chopped parsley sprinkled on top.

Cousin Mary-Ann (King) DiPietro's Penne, Chicken & Broccoli

This is a recipe cousin Mary-Ann has created. It's something she likes to make for her family and they love it.

1 bunch broccoli florets

3 cloves of finely chopped garlic

2 tbsp. olive oil

½ cup chicken broth

Salt and pepper

2 chicken breast cut into pieces

1 lb. penne pasta

Cook pasta until al dente. Save a cup of starchy water to add when getting ready to finish the dish. Take all the other above ingredients, which you've put in a large pan or wok to briefly cook in the olive oil, then add the chicken broth, add your pasta with a little of the starch water. Mix all together and add a pat of butter.

Sprinkle some grated cheese and some red pepper flakes.

Cousin Ann Grondalski's Special Pork Loin

This is a recipe my cousin Ann has loved to make. It's a little sweet, a little tangy. Just perfect!

1 4-5 lb. boneless pork loin

½ cup olive oil

1 tbsp. finely chopped basil

Salt & pepper

2 tsp garlic powder

½ cup red wine

½ cup teriyaki marinade

Mix all ingredients in a bowl to create a nice "rub" for the pork. Once all are combined in a bowl, place your pork loin in a baking dish and take your rub/marinade and rub all over the loin. Cook at 375 degress for approximately 45 minutes-1 hour or until done.

Fettucine Carbonara

This is a classic Italian dish that Nonie absolutely loved to make for us to eat. It was not one that was regularly on the menu at Ciro's, but when we had a craving for it, the chef would make it, just like she had taught him.

1 lb. fettucine pasta

4-5 slices of cooked crisp bacon

½ stick butter

2 eggs

1 cup grated parmesean cheese

2 cloves garlic

A handful of fresh chopped parsley

Salt & pepper

1 cup heavy cream

Boil the pasta until al dente. Transfer to a large frying pan, with butter melting. Add your chopped crisp bacon slices. In a bowl beat the 2 eggs, finely chopped garlic, and add the parmesan cheese as well as the salt and pepper and heavy cream, and slowly pour over the pasta that is in the frying pan. Combine and toss well. The mixture with the fettucine will be thick and creamy. Garnish with the fresh parsley.

Sausage with Onions, Potatoes, and Peppers

This is a classic Italian meal. I can see Dad with the big frying pan making this yummy (and very easy) recipe! You can use with hot or sweet Italian sausage. He usually used sweet, or sometimes mixed both!

1-2 lbs. sweet or hot Italian sausage links

1 large white onions sliced in big chunks

1 -2 large sliced green peppers

4-6 potatoes cut in chunks

2 tbsp. olive oil

2 or 3 pats of butter

3-4 chopped garlic cloves

Salt & pepper

Peel and boil potatoes, then let cool and cut into chunks. In a large frying pan add oil, a couple pats of butter for added flavor, garlic, and add the potatoes with the sausage to start browning on all sides. Add the onions and peppers. Sauté until fully cooked. The vegetables should be slightly firm, not too soft.

Cousin Alberto's Eggplant Parmesan

I have fond memories of Dad and Nonie making a big pan of Eggplant Parmesan. We all loved it. This is how Alberto makes it. He likes to cut his eggplant lengthwise, where I cut it in circles. It's all your own preference.

3-4 eggplants

3 eggs

¼ cup flour

½ cup Italian bread crumbs

1 container ricotta cheese

1 large bag of mozzarella shredded cheese

Parmigiana grated cheese

Olive oil

Peel and cut eggplants into lengthwise strips approximately 1/8th of an inch or slightly thicker. Dip pieces in flour, then eggs which are beaten, then in Italian bread crumbs. Make sure your flour and breadcrumbs are seasoned with salt, pepper, and garlic powder.

Begin to fry in hot olive oil in large frying pan, and once they are browned drain them on paper bags or towels to remove excess oil.

Line a casserole dish with your favorite sauce and begin layering the eggplant. Sprinkle parmigiana cheese, mozzarella, and some ricotta on top and begin layering process again. Bake at 375 degrees until cheese is bubbly and melted.

Dad's Chicken with Peas and Potatoes

This is probably one of the easiest, but tastiest dishes Dad loved to make in the back kitchen of the Blue Room banquet room at Ciro's. His "secret" for extra flavor was adding little chunks of salt pork.

2-3 lbs. skin on/bone in chicken thighs and or legs

1-2 lbs. diced potatoes

1-2 large white diced onions

2 bags frozen peas

½ lb. diced salt pork for flavor

5 or 6 crushed cloves of garlic

Olive oil

Salt & pepper.

Sauté in olive oil the diced potatoes, onion, and salt pork. On a large baking sheet, add some olive oil. To that add your chicken pieces, and your potatoes, onions, salt pork, and roast in a 425 degrees for approximately an hour. Every once and a while check how things are cooking and flip everything to assure browning and crisp skin is forming on chicken. Last 15 minutes or so add the frozen peas. This will prevent them from getting mushy (that's why canned peas are not recommended). Serve on a large platter for "family style" eating!

Shrimp Scampi

My family ate a lot of fish and not just at Christmas. Many dishes we love such as shrimp scampi were served at Ciro's also. The clientele loved it as much as we did. It was usually served with linguine pasta. It's a very light, lovely dish.

24 U-10 size shrimp

Large handful of fresh parsley chopped

1-2 whole lemons cut in wedges

1 stick of butter

1 cup white wine

6-8 cloves chopped garlic

1 small white onion diced fine

Olive oil

Salt & pepper

Rinse, peel, and devein the shrimp so the black vein that runs in the back is completely removed. Set aside. Put some olive oil and ½ of a stick of butter in a large frying pan, and add the chopped garlic and the finely diced onion. While this is sautéing it will become transparent (and the smell will be incredible!). Add your shimp, the juice of one lemon, the wine, half the parsley ,and the rest of the butter.

The shrimp will only take a few minutes to cook. Finally add the remaining parsley, salt and pepper, and serve over your favorite pasta. Add additional lemon wedges around the platter.

Angel Hair Pasta with Anchovy Sauce

This is a traditional recipe my family always made during the "Feast of the Seven Fishes" on Christmas Eve. I can still see Nonie's large kitchen and dining room table filled with all the foods for that evening. It's a memory I will never forget. Dad and Aunt Rose would be running around getting everything ready. Christmas Eves have never been the same since those days; partially because of the food, but mostly because I can no longer actually experience those times, only in memory.

2-3 lb. boxes of Angel Hair Pasta

¼ cup olive oil

2 can anchovy fillets

1/3 cup chicken stock (preferably homemade)

1/3 cup pignoli (pine nuts)

Chopped parsley (optional)

4-5 smashed cloves of garlic

In a large pasta pot, add plenty of salt and drop the pasta in when water comes to a rolling boil. Angel hair pasta is very thin and fine, so it will only take a few moments to cook (2-4 minutes).

In the meantime, add olive oil, along with garlic, some parsley if you like and drop in the anchovies. Slowly add your stock as this is bubbling and cook over a medium high heat.This heat will make them dissolve and create a wonderful sauce within a few minutes.

After having pulled out the Angel Hair from the salted water (don't rinse) add directly to the large frying pan, into the oil, garlic, anchovy sauce. Add pine nuts and toss. Place in a large bowl, garnish with remaining parsley and serve! Cousin Alberto reminded me to make sure to tell you all that the Angel Hair pasta soaks up the sauce like crazy, so be sure to make enough for it!

Cousin Carla (Stone) Sarno's Fillet of Sole Francaise

There are a few of Carla's recipes that she frequently makes for her 2 lovely daughters and her husband Dominic, the Mayor of the City of Springfield. This fillet of sole is so easy and so tasty.

3-4 lbs. fillet of sole or any white fish like cod

Flour for breading fish

4 eggs beaten

Salt & pepper

Chopped fresh parsley

1 stick butter

1 cup of chicken stock

4 cloves crushed garlic

2 whole lemons

Zest of 1 lemon

Season the flour with salt, black pepper, and chopped parsley in a 9x13" pan. Take the beaten eggs, put in a shallow bowl. Flour the fish segments, and then dip them in the eggs. Have a frying pan with a couple tablespoons of olive oil getting hot, and place the fish in the frying pan. Once golden brown, take out and set aside in a baking dish. Discard excess oil from pan, and return to heat. Add one stick of butter and let melt, one can of College Inn chicken broth or homemade stock, chopped garlic, the juice of 2 lemons, lemon zest, and parsley.

Heat through, then pour the sauce over the fish and bake in oven at 350 degrees for 15 minutes. Once it is heated through, sprinkle parsley flakes and serve with additional lemon wedges. If you make enough sauce, Carla says to make Angel Hair pasta to serve with it.

Cousin Alberto's Easter Lamb Shanks

Although Alberto made this dish on Easter Sunday for him and his family, it can be made anytime because it's considered a "Dutch oven" all in one meal!

1 lamb shank

5-6 carrots sliced

5-6 leeks (rinsed well and sliced

1 quart chicken stock

2 Spanish onions diced

1 -2 cups white wine

2-3 cups of tomato sauce or canned crushed tomatoes

15 or so cloves of garlic

Salt and pepper the lamb, and add a few tablespoons of olive oil to a Dutch oven and brown on all sides. Take the lamb out and add the garlic, carrots, onions, and leeks. Cook these until soft, then add a cup of wine, the chicken stock, and the tomato sauce and bring back up to a boil.

Cover and put in the oven at 375 degrees for 2-3 hours, or until the meat begins to fall off the bone.

Serve with potatoes and vegetable of choice.

Cousin Carla (Stone) Sarno's Beef Tenderloin Marsala

Beef Marsala is one of Carla's favorite dishes to make. It makes a lovely Sunday supper meal.

4 rib eye or 6 beef tenderloin Steaks (seasoned with salt and pepper)

1 stick butter

2-4 tablespoons Olive Oil

2-3 cloves of garlic

1 cup of Marsala wine

2 packages of sliced baby bella mushrooms (portabella)

2 tablespoons flour

Sear steaks that have been seasoned on both sides with salt and pepper in a frying pan with a drizzle of olive oil and half a stick of butter and garlic which has been minced. Cook to rare. Remove from pan and set aside. Do not drain pan.

Add the sliced mushrooms, the remaining half stick of butter, and a drizzle more olive oil. Sauté. Add Marsala wine and let reduce. Add flour gradually, while stirring mixture to let it thicken into a nice sauce.

Place the steaks on an oven safe serving platter, and top them with the mushroom Marsala sauce in a 350-degree oven for approximately 10 minutes.

If you like, it pairs very well with some rosemary sprinkled on top with some roasted fingerling potatoes on the side.

Linguine with White Clam Sauce

At Ciro's you could choose this dish with either white clam sauce or with red sauce with clams. To me, the "white clam sauce" was always light and delicious, the red a bit spicy.

5 dozen small little neck or manila clams, scrubbed well under water

10 cloves garlic minced

1 cup white wine

Olive oil

1-2 dashes of crushed red pepper flakes (optional)

1 lb. linguine

2 tablespoons butter

½ bunch of Italian parsley chopped

2 tablespoons oregano

Salt & pepper

In a large sauté pan add a few tablespoons of olive oil and about half of the minced garlic.

Cook the garlic just until golden brown. Add approximately 3 and a half dozen or so of the clams, add the wine and a half cup water. Cover and cook until the clams open.

Remove the clams from the pan and reduce the liquid which is left. Once the clams are slightly cooled, remove them from their shells, discard the shells, and pour the reduced liquid into a cup. At this point, you can chop the clams to add to your sauce later on.

Coating the same sauté pan again with more olive oil, add the remaining garlic, and a pinch of red pepper flakes, if desired. Add the remaining raw clams and the reserved cooking liquid. Once again cover and cook until remaining clams have opened.

Remove the clams from the pan once again and set aside. Do not take out of shell or chop.

To a boiling pot of water, with added salt, drop linguine pasta to cook.

Add butter and chopped clams back to the pan and bring the liquid to a boil, and toss with your al dente linguine. Add remaining herbs, and place the clams in the shells on top of the finished dish. Drizzle with a good amount of olive oil. Add salt and pepper to taste.

Serve with fresh Italian bread! Serves 4

Baked Rigatoni with Ricotta and Mozzarella

What could be easier than making a bubbling dish of baked rigatoni? It's a classic dish, and the success was the using the exact ratio of ricotta and mozzarella. Our homemade red sauce also gave it the wonderful flavor that Ciro's customers loved!

2 lbs. rigatoni

2 quarts red sauce, with or without meat

4 beaten eggs

2 large containers ricotta cheese

4-6 cups shredded mozzarella cheese

1 cup grated parmesan cheese

1 tablespoon Italian Seasoning or just plain Oregano

Heavily salt a pot of water and bring to boil. Drop rigatoni into the pot and cook according to the package. Preheat oven to 350 degrees.

In a large bowl, combine beaten eggs, ricotta cheese, Italian seasoning, 3 cups mozzarella and a half cup parmesan cheese. Coat the bottom of a large baking dish with some olive oil and add enough of your favorite sauce to the bottom to cover the whole dish.

Drain your al dente rigatoni and begin layering the pasta first, then the cheese mixture, then another layer of sauce. Make sure you add enough sauce, and cheese over the pasta, so it does not come out dry. Pasta "soaks" up the sauce. Layer until the top of the baking dish is filled. Finally heavily sprinkle 3 cups or so of the mozzarella and remaining parmesan. Bake for 45 minutes or until the cheese is golden and bubbling.

Be sure to let it stand and "set up" for 10 or 15 minutes before cutting into it. Serve with a salad and some Italian bread.

Chicken a la Cacciatore

If you like red sauce, chicken, and mushrooms, you will love this "hunter's stew." This is another Ciro's classic.

1 3-4lb chicken cut into serving pieces (legs, thighs, breast) bone in, skin on

2 cloves minced garlic

1 sprig rosemary leaves only, minced very fine

2 large onions coarsely chopped

1lb of portobello or white mushrooms cut into large pieces

¼ lb. pancetta, diced

Olive oil

Salt and pepper

6 ribs celery cut into one-inch pieces

3 cups basic tomato sauce

1 cup white wine

To the 3-4 tablespoons of olive oil add minced garlic, about ½ of the finely chopped rosemary, salt and pepper in a large bowl to make a "paste." Take chicken pieces and gently massage the mixture all over the chicken parts evenly. If you can refrigerate at least a few hours that would be fine.

Using a large Dutch oven add another 3-4 tablespoons of olive oil, making sure it's very hot. Add the chicken pieces (don't crowd the Dutch oven) and brown on all sides. Remove chicken and transfer to some paper towels to absorb excess grease.

Add the diced pancetta, celery, mushrooms and onions to the Dutch oven and cook them until the pancetta has rendered down and vegetables are fork tender, approximately 10 minutes. Add the wine and the tomato sauce and stir all ingredients. Bring it to a boil. Return the chicken pieces to the Dutch oven, then cover and lower the heat to simmer and cook an additional 20-30 minutes, until all flavors are incorporated.

Spaghetti a la Ciro

This is a unique Ciro's recipe that was on the menu throughout the years. You would never think to use mushrooms with spaghetti! So delicious.

1-2 lb. spaghetti

Olive oil

3 cloves garlic minced

3 cups of your favorite sauce

11/2 cup presliced mushrooms

Add salt to a large pot of water and bring to a boil. Add spaghetti and cook according to package, or until al dente. In a sauté pan add olive oil and garlic, and then add mushrooms to cook. If you like, you can even use precooked jarred sliced mushroom, drained off the liquid.

Once spaghetti is cooked, add it to the tomato sauce, then add the mushrooms and toss. Enjoy.

Lauren's version of Stuffed Peppers

When I was growing up, and we weren't at Ciro's, we would often make a wonderful mixture that we would stuff into green peppers, zucchini boats or even large portobello mushroom caps. Traditionally, we would use a mixture that included ground beef and pork with rice, but over the years I have experimented and have found I just love the taste of using ground turkey with a few "secret" ingredients. Everyone raves about it when I serve it. Most of the time they don't even know it's ground turkey (not that that's a bad thing!!)

4-6 green bell peppers or zucchini, cut lengthwise

10-12 giant portobello mushroom caps

2-3 lbs. ground turkey

1 egg beaten

1 large onion diced

½ cup grated parmesan cheese

2-3 dashes Worcestershire sauce

2-3 dashes soy sauce

1 -2 cups white rice

Garlic, salt & black pepper

1 quart red sauce

Shredded mozzarella cheese

Whether using bell peppers, zucchini or giant Portobello mushroom caps, each vessel must be cleaned and any seeds or stems be discarded. In the case of a bell pepper, I usually cut them lengthwise and clean the ribs and seeds; zucchini, cut lengthwise as well, and inner "flesh" cleaned out with a spoon, so boat is formed. Not much needs to be done to the mushroom, unless the stem is still present. If it is, just gently break it off from the cap.

Cook the rice according to the package. Add anywhere between 1 and 2 cups of rice, depending on how much of a meat to rice ratio you would like. Let rice cool once cooked.

In a large bowl, add raw ground turkey, egg for binding purposes, chopped onion, Worcestershire and soy, salt, pepper, and garlic, and some grated parmesan cheese and mix. Once rice is cooled, add rice to mixture.

In the bottom of a large baking dish cover the bottom with a coating of red sauce and begin stuffing your vegetables. Once all are in the dish sprinkle a bit more grated cheese and a good amount of shredded mozzarella cheese. Add a bit more sauce amongst the vegetables, cover and place in a 350-degree oven for about 45 minutes. When almost done, remove foil and place under the broiler to brown up the melted cheese on the top.

Lemon Chicken (or Veal) Piccata on Angel Hair Pasta

Ciro's made the best chicken or veal piccata, because they used to pound the cutlets very thin and made a lush lemon cream sauce with sounds heavy, but was very light. I have added the angel hair pasta as an accompaniment, although you pretty much could pair it with any starch and or vegetable.

4-6 boneless chicken cutlets or veal cutlets

½ cup flour, seasoned with salt and pepper

3-4 tablespoons butter

2-3 tablespoons olive oil

1/1/2 cup chicken stock

2 lemons

¾ cup heavy cream

¼-¼ cup capers

¼ cup white wine

Fresh chopped parsley and 1 lb. Angel hair pasta cooked according to package

In a large pot begin boiling heavily salted water for the pasta. Take chicken and or veal cutlets and lightly pound them until they are nice and thin. Dredge them in seasoned flour. In a large skillet, let butter melt in oil until bubbling. Gently place either protein in skillet and cook until golden brown on both sides, 4-5 minutes. Remove from pan and set aside on a plate.

Turn down the heat to medium and add the juice of lemons, the chicken stock, white wine, heavy cream, and capers. Bring the sauce to a boil, and then return to medium heat. Add salt and pepper if needed. Capers are very salty (Cousin Alberto and I love them). Be sure to taste the sauce, so it's not too salty and to your liking.

Add the protein back into the sauce. By this time the pasta will be cooked. Pull pasta from pot and place into a large serving bowl. Pour the sauce and place the chicken or veal on top. Sprinkle with a generous amount of fresh chopped parsley. If pasta seems to have "soaked up all the sauce" add a half cup or so of the salted starchy water from the pasta you just boiled.

Sweets

My family really didn't bake much. I think the reason was that there were such wonderful Italian bakery shops like La Fiorentina Bakery, which was (and still is) right across the street. There are a few recipes that Nonie and my Dad made from time to time, as well as some nice cookie recipes from Cousin Ann Grondalski, as well as a few from Nana Siemienkowicz.

Nonie's Zabaglione (Marsala Custard)

This dessert has only 3 ingredients, but quite delicious!

6 egg yolks

½ cup sugar

1 cup Marsala wine

Beat the eggs and sugar until thick and lemon-colored. Stir in the wine. Cook the mixture in the top of a double boiler over simmering water. Beat constantly with a rotary beater until mixture is very light and begins to thicken. When the mixture begins to rise, remove from heat. Serve hot or cold, with a dab of whipped cream in a pretty glass. Serves 6.

St. Joseph Day Zeppoli (Italian Fried Bread Dough)

Italian-Americans always celebrate St. Joseph Day, a Christian holiday which is March 19th. Foods are traditionally served containing bread "crumbs" to represent sawdust since St. Joseph was a carpenter. It was a time we looked forward to after eating our dinner at Ciro's because it also was Papa's birthday. Dad would be in the back kitchen frying the dough, then serving it to us, loaded with sugar sprinkled on top.

1 package active dry yeast

1 cup water

1 1/2 cups all-purpose flour

1 quart of vegetable oil for frying

2 tablespoons either granulated or confectioner's sugar

Heat 3 or 4 inches of oil in a deep sauce pan. Dissolve yeast in a half cup warm water in a large bowl and set aside for 10 minutes. Stir remaining half cup of water into the bowl. Add flour beating vigorously until a soft dough forms. Turn dough out onto a smooth surface, and knead with greased hands until it is smooth.

Place the dough in a greased bowl and turn to coat the surface. Cover with a damp cloth.

Let rise in a warm place until it doubles in size, about 1-1/2 hours. Roll the dough out into small round disks (approx. 4-5") in diameter. Drop into oil and fry in batches until golden brown

Drain on paper towels and while hot, sprinkle sugar and enjoy!

Cousin Ann Grondalski's Jeanett Cookies

The following two cookie recipes come straight from my cousin's handwritten recipe box!

This is the first one.

Cookie recipe

1 cup of Crisco (from the can)

1 1/2 cup sugar

4 large eggs

1 cup orange juice

1 teaspoon each orange and lemon extract

1 teaspoon baking soda

6 teaspoons baking powder

6 cups flour

Frosting

1 cup confectioner's sugar

4-6 tablespoons water

½ teaspoon lemon extract

Mix the Crisco, sugar, and eggs in a large bowl with a mixer until incorporated. Add the orange juice, extracts, baking soda, baking powder, flour, and mix all together well.

Drop by teaspoon on a nonstick cookie sheet and bake at 400 degrees for 12 minutes.

Let cool. Mix the ingredients for the frosting together until it has reached a thin consistency. Then drizzle over the cookies. You can add colored sprinkles if you like to make them more festive!

Cousin Ann's Fruit Cocktail Cookies

1/2 cup softened butter

½ cup sugar

½ cup light brown sugar, firmly packed

1 jumbo egg, beaten

½ teaspoon vanilla

¼ teaspoon almond extract

1 1/2 cup all-purpose flour

½ teaspoon baking soda and baking powder

½ teaspoon cinnamon

¼ teaspoon ground cloves

1/8th teaspoon salt

1 cup canned fruit cocktail drained well

½ cup raisins

Preheat oven to 375 degrees. Grease and flour baking sheets.

Cream butter with sugar and add brown sugar. Add beaten egg, extracts, and beat until smooth.

Mix all dry ingredients in a medium bowl and mix into it the butter mixture. Stir in fruit cocktail and raisins. Drop by heaping teaspoons onto cookie sheets. Bake 11-12 minutes or until lightly golden brown. Transfer to wire rack to cool. This makes about 5 dozen cookies.

Nana Siemienkowicz's 1950s Pineapple Upside Down Cake

I felt it wouldn't be right if I didn't add a few of my Nana's very simple but delicious sweet recipes. Perhaps the next book will be an ode to her and her recipes? She was not of Italian descent, but a wonderful (and very typical) Polish-American grandma. If you're Polish, you know exactly what I mean! I have such fond memories baking with her. She always let me "lick the spoon," and we had a lot of fun times!

¼ cup softened butter

¼ cup packed light brown sugar

1 8 ounce can of pineapple slices, drained

½ cup original Bisquick mix

½ cup granulated sugar

½ cup milk

2 tbsp. vegetable oil

1 tsp. vanilla extract

1 egg

Preheat oven to 350 degrees. In a 9-inch round pan, melt the butter in the oven and sprinkle the brown sugar over the melted butter. Arrange the pineapple slices in a single layer over the sugar mixture.

In a large bowl, beat remaining ingredients with an electric hand mixer on low speed for approximately 30-40 seconds. Scrape the bowl, and then resume beating on medium speed for 4 minutes. Pour the batter over the pineapples and bake for 35-40 minutes or until toothpick inserted in center comes out clean.

Place a heatproof serving plate upside down over pan, turn plate and pan over. Leave the pan over the cake a few minutes then remove and cool for 10 minutes. This makes 8 servings.

Nana Siemienkowicz's 1940s Peanut Butter Cookies

Nana loved peanut butter, even on a piece of plain old white bread! She taught me how to make these simple cookies. I remember taking them to school for many of the bake sales we would have. The fondest memories attached to this recipe is how she taught me to take a fork and press down on the cookie dough before baking to make a pretty "design" on top.

½ cup creamy peanut butter

½ cup butter

½ cup granulated sugar

½ cup brown sugar, firmly packed

1 large egg, beaten

11/4 cup flour

¾ teaspoon baking soda

½ teaspoon baking powder

¼ teaspoon salt

Preheat oven to 375 degrees. Cream butter and peanut butter together and add the sugar gradually. Add the beaten egg and sift the flour once before measuring it. Then sift the flour, baking soda and powder and salt together. Add to the creamed mixture. Chill dough for at least an hour.

Once chilled, roll the dough into balls the size of a walnut and place them on a lightly greased baking sheet. Flatten with a fork dipped in flour, making crisscross pattern. Bake 10-12 minutes.

Makes 4 dozen

Nana Siemienkowicz's Jam Thumbprint Cookies

This was a fun recipe because you can use whatever kind of jam you have in your refrigerator at that moment. Nana loved to use seedless raspberry, apricot or strawberry jam. This is a recipe she told me she had made back in the 1950s for my Grandpa Eddie and my Mom! She passed it on to me.

2 cups flour

2 teaspoons baking powder

1 cup butter, softened

1 cup sugar

1 large egg

1 teaspoon vanilla extract

¼ cup milk

About a cup of jam of your choice

Preheat oven to 350 degrees. Grease 2 baking sheets. In a large bowl, beat butter with sugar, add egg, and vanilla. Beat well until smooth. Mix in flour and baking powder and add milk.

Mix very well. Refrigerate for 15 minutes before using.

Roll the dough when chilled into tablespoon size balls and place on baking sheets. Make a "well" in each ball with your thumb. Fill the well with your favorite jam.

Bake for 15-18 minutes, or until they begin to brown. Cool on baking sheets before transferring to wire racks to cool completely.

Makes 3 dozen

Lauren's Tiramisu Trifle

You don't have to be Italian to love Tiramisu! I make many trifles and this is always a crowd pleaser. It's very similar to the actual Tiramisu cake, but as a layered dessert with creamy mascarpone cheese and pudding it's very light and delicious!

½ -3/4 cup Espresso or very strong coffee

¼ cup of amaretto liqueur or a coffee liqueur (which ever you prefer)

1 regular size container of mascarpone cheese

2 containers of cool whip

2 boxes of instant vanilla pudding, prepared

1 sponge cake or 3 packages of lady finger sponge cakes

4 or 5 ounces of shaved dark or milk chocolate for top of trifle

10-12 fresh raspberries (optional)

Prepare the pudding according to package and refrigerate for a couple hours to set up.

In a pretty trifle bowl, break up with your hands the sponge cake or line the bottom with lady fingers. Mix the coffee (cool) with the liqueur of your choice and drizzle over the bottom layer of sponge cake, so it soaks up the flavor.

Fold the mascarpone cheese into the pudding and mix together until smooth. Being layering all ingredients, first with the pudding mixture on top of the soaked sponge cake, then a layer of cool whip. Repeat at least 2 -3 times until all ingredients are used. The top of the trifle should end with the cool whip, and then sprinkle the chocolate shavings generously on top. If you like, you can also add a few raspberries on top for garnish with the chocolate. It may seem "healthier" that way! Serve cold, at least a few hours if not overnight. Enjoy!